A CAREER IN THE HORSE INDUSTRY 1995-1996

LAURA COLLINS

Kenilworth Press

First published 1994 by
The Kenilworth Press Ltd
Addington
Buckingham MK18 2JR

British Library Cataloguing in Publication Data
A catalogue record for this book is available from the British Library

ISBN 1-872082-63-7

Design by Paul Saunders
Typeset in Times 11/13.5
Typesetting and layout by The Kenilworth Press Ltd
Printed in Great Britain by Redwood Books, Trowbridge

Contents

Foreword by Jeremy Houghton Brown 5
Acknowledgements 6
Introduction 7

1 Planning Your Career in the Horse Industry 9
2 Riding Instructors and Grooms 19
3 Further Opportunities 44
4 The Racing Industry 64
5 The Field of Medicine 85
6 Job Hunting and Employment 103
7 Self-Employment 114
8 Training 132

Useful addresses 155
Index 158

For Mum –
Thank you for Ambassador

Foreword

by Jeremy Houghton Brown B Phil Ed
Principal Lecturer in Equine Studies, Warwickshire College

Anyone planning to work with horses, or even thinking about such a possibility, should read this book.

Knowledge is a precious thing and this book gives real in-depth insight into the jobs and careers in the horse industry. Not only is it well researched but the many interviews depict it the way it really is. There is no gloss; people tell of their experiences both good and bad. However, shining through comes the great love of horses and the horse world which is the key to all aspects of the work. Personal pride, willingness to work hard and achieve high standards – these are common themes. Academic or intensely practical, there are jobs and careers for all.

Those of us who work in the horse industry would not change our world for any other. Those who think they might like to join us need to read this book; it unravels the maze yet makes good reading.

Jeremy Houghton Brown

Acknowledgements

Many people generously helped in my research for this book, especially: the secretaries and staff of the various horse associations and colleges, including the staff in the training offices of the British Horse Society and its director, John Goldsmith; the Association of British Riding Schools; the National Pony Society; the Thoroughbred Breeder's Association; the National Stud; the Jockey Club; the staff, both past and present, at the JNHETC, in particular Jeremy Houghton Brown, who has taken so much time and trouble to read my manuscript, and marketing consultant, Alan Newton; the Lord O'Hagan MEP, his secretary and researchers.

Much of the information included in this book comes 'direct from the horse's mouth'. I am greatly indebted to the following: David Broome, and his head groom Emma Storey; Mary Thomson, and her head girl Annie Collings; Mary Tyrell and Ted Moore of the TM School of Horsemanship in Cornwall; globe trotter Josephine Tyack; Tim Keyte, of Hunters Polo Yard in Cirencester; Alexandria Smith, horse dealer; Kathleen Connor, BHSAI; Vanessa Cheffing and Kerry Hutchings of Downe Farm Dressage Training Yard in Devon.

In racing I owe much to the hospitality and knowledge imparted by Peter Compton, Training and Education Officer for the National Trainers Federation and the British Racing Schools; Sue and Jim Gale of the Northern Racing School; apprentices of the British Racing School; Bill Adams, National Secretary of the Stable Lads Association.

My thanks also go to Dawn McHugh at the Animal Health Clinic, Newmarket; David Buckley at the Mullacot Veterinary Hospital, Devon; Ann Longden, physiotherapist; Sarah Kendal, McTimoney Chiropractor.

Finally, a special thank you must go to my husband, Richard, for his stoical support, and to my son, Rhyan, for keeping a smile on my face.

Introduction

Ambition makes the difference between just working with horses, and having a career in the horse industry. Whether you're a school leaver, an experienced groom, or someone who has been made redundant from another profession, this book has been written to help you to plan a successful career structure in the horse industry by giving you a real insight into working with horses. Forget the over-worked and under-paid image that others may use to discourage you. From racing to riding schools, the horse industry can offer you: excellent training, promotion, good pay, free accommodation, and the opportunity to travel within the UK and abroad.

Including the experience and advice of both employees and employers currently in the industry, this book will help you get the most out of your career with horses. If you are currently working in the horse industry and feel disillusioned, then it will help you re-direct your career aims to achieve the success and job satisfaction you desire. By reading about the experiences of others, you'll stand a better chance of avoiding some of the pitfalls of working with horses.

If you have recently been made redundant from a job unconnected with horses, and have always wanted to work with horses, remember that the skills and confidence you have achieved in your previous career will be of great use in your new venture. Don't let your lack of experience with horses deter you; there are plenty of opportunities to improve and expand your knowledge. This book also includes advice and information for the disabled and for overseas students.

To work directly with horses you need to be physically fit and strong, not afraid of hard work, and have a calm temperament – horses are sensitive to your moods, and a quiet disposition goes a long way to having calm, contented horses.

Training is important. Qualifications will give you the edge over other applicants. A prospective employer will know that you can work and ride to the required standard and can cope under pressure – essential qualities for working in today's professional yard. The training you choose should reflect your ultimate aims. There is little point in taking the BHS Instructors examinations if you have no desire to teach. If your goal in life is to run your own livery or dealing yard, many colleges include courses that teach you business skills as well equestrianism.

Finding the right job with horses can be a daunting task. Until you find a job that is suitable, don't demean the ones you are offered. Sometimes a job that doesn't pay well offers compensation by providing professional tuition or opportunities for foreign travel. Jobs that offer you the chance to compete greatly increase your confidence and experience, giving you the vital skills to go for that 'management' position or to set up your own business.

Whatever you choose to do with horses, bear in mind the frequent lament of employers that, 'good grooms are like gold dust.' All too often, grooms are put off working with horses because of a bad employer, and consequently turn their ability for hard work and exacting standards to other industries. Please don't be put off – bad employers are not unique to the horse industry, they exist in all walks of life. Today, most employers accept that proper training and wages are essential in attracting good workers into the industry.

Working in the horse industry doesn't necessarily mean direct work with horses, and this book includes many alternatives which you may not previously have thought about or weren't quite sure how to get into. With the right qualifications and good references, you can achieve whatever goal you desire. It is up to you to make the best of your talents, and the wider experience gained by working in different aspects of the industry will give you a solid foundation on which to build your own enterprise – this is not as far out of reach as you may think!

Finally, do not describe yourself as simply wishing to work with horses, but state that you want *a career in the horse industry*, because that is what this book is all about. Ambition, dedication, talent and a willingness to work hard are the essential qualities of success in any career. If you possess these qualities, you'll go far!

Chapter 1

Planning Your Career in the Horse Industry

With a total annual turnover of £60 million and an estimated 250,000 people employed in this industry, horses should not be overlooked as a career prospect. The British Government now recognises that horses have an important role in the British economy – the industry now has its own government minister to watch over and help it. In the past, investors, employers and employees were left to fend for themselves, leaving us far behind our European counterparts who have for many years been recognised and aided by their governments.

Perhaps improvements in economic policy will allow the horse industry to prosper, and conditions for those employed in the industry will be improved, so that the British horse world will maintain and enhance its reputation. British horseracing and Thoroughbred breeding have an excellent reputation, which is of importance to our economy.

The British Thoroughbred has also made a contribution of enormous significance in producing horses outstanding in competitions, showing and hunting. Similarly, the many native breed societies have played an important role, not only in preserving and improving native horses and ponies, but also in supporting amateur and professional breeders and competitors. All these activities contribute to the economy as a whole. Above all, we are indebted to the hard work and dedication of our grooms and riders – Britain's greatest ambassadors for the horse industry.

The horse industry can be divided into three parts:

The *racing* or *Thoroughbred industry* is popular not only with horse lovers, but also with a wider public through televised racing and gambling. Racing is the only aspect of direct work with horses where there is a statutory (though not mandatory) pay scheme. As well as work in a racing stable, this industry also includes associated jobs such as administration, transport, racecourse management and Thoroughbred breeding. For those aspiring to be jockeys or stable lads, there are now two excellent racing schools that teach the riding and stable management skills required in this type of work.

The *non-Thoroughbred industry* encompasses all sorts of jobs that involve working with horses 'hands-on', including grooms, riders, instructors, stable managers, travelling grooms and stud employees. Training can now be undertaken at an agricultural college or an equestrian centre, or you can combine both.

Horse-associated activities include saddlery, farriery, veterinary care, feed merchants, insurance agencies, tack shops, horse society and trade organisation staff, riding clothes manufacturers, stable and equipment manufacturers, journalists, publishers, sales staff, agents, abattoirs, auctioneers – the list seems endless but there are many people in related activities who rely on horses for a living.

If you are planning to work as a groom for only a short time, or don't want to be involved directly with horses at all, you could consider your long-term career prospects in one of these related areas. However, your knowledge and experience of working with horses will go a long way to helping you gain employment and achieve success.

PLANNING YOUR CAREER

Even if you are still at school, it is not too early to be thinking about a career plan. You've already made up your mind that you want to work with horses and once you've read this book, you'll have a fair idea what aspect of work will best suit your talents and personality.

It's worth remembering, for example, that a groom's work is both physically and emotionally demanding and grooms can often 'burn themselves out' after a few years. They then move into other careers without making full use of all the equine skills and knowledge they have acquired. If you're clever, you will use your school education to your long-term advantage to help you gain employment in a horse-associated job. That may seem a long way off at the moment, and not worth worrying about because you don't think that you will ever giving up working with horses, but heed the advice of show jumper David Broome:

'Working as a professional groom means a lot of hard graft. There are many rewards to the job – you see the world if you're in a top yard. However, there is a limit to where you can go in groom's work and it's certainly not something you want to be doing when you're forty; it's for the young and the fit! Don't see it as your only option.'

David's head groom, Emma Storey, agrees:

'You've really got to have something else behind you. You should concentrate on exams and education whilst still at school because you've got to have qualifications to do something else, even if it is still associated with horses, like marketing or veterinary work. Groom's work is a short life because it is such a physical life. A lot of people don't realise that.'

'Good grooms are like gold dust,' is the frequent lament of employers. By 'good grooms' they mean people who are hard-working, sensible and dedicated. If you have trouble getting out of bed in the morning, you don't like doing anything that is physically exhausting, or you don't care about standards and would rather be doing something that doesn't require strength, pride and perseverance, then it is likely that you will quickly become disillusioned with groom's work. It works both ways; good employers deserve good grooms.

You should decide early on whether you are really cut out to be a groom. If you don't think that you are, or you prefer to keep riding as a hobby, then perhaps you should consider working in a horse-related activity such as saddlery, medicine or secretarial work. Many grooms take up these sort of associated jobs as they can be just as enjoyable, and often better paid!

To succeed in any career you've got to have the right attitude towards work and people, and of course you must also genuinely love horses, because they can be as difficult to work with as humans. There is a big difference between looking after the daily needs of your own horse or pony and looking after three or four show jumpers or racehorses every day. Although both are fun and challenging, a job involves working a lot harder for much longer hours and you can't get your mum to do it if you want to go away for the weekend!

If you've helped out at your local riding school, you'll have a fair idea of the hard work involved and just how tired you'll be at the end of the day. If you've never helped out and just attended for lessons, it would be wise to ask if you can stay for the day and help the staff – then you'll know whether you can cope. Working in a riding school involves the longest hours and hardest 'graft' for the poorest pay. On the other hand, most professional yards have some sort of timetable to stick to, so you won't have to deal with the public on such a large scale and there may be opportunities for better pay.

If you enjoy helping out at your local school and thrive on physical challenge, then you'll enjoy working as a groom. Some riding schools rely heavily on the voluntary help of school kids at weekends; the better organised ones make sure they have adequate staff to cover the extra work. There's nothing wrong with helping out at your local riding school, but because teachers, parents and careers officers are usually only familiar with this part of the horse industry, they take the view that all work with horses is as exploitative.

WHILE STILL AT SCHOOL

Your Riding and Horse Knowledge

If you are lucky enough to have your own horse or pony, you should still ride as much as you can under tuition because you never stop learning when it comes to horses – that's one of the attractions of this career. Join your local Pony or Riding Club – you don't need to be a horse owner – and you can take their progressive tests. The BHS (British Horse Society) also offers a system of exams for horse owners. The Horse Owner's Certificates Stages I to III will not only encourage you and help you to take better care of your horse or pony, but will also provide a sound basis on which to commence your BHS training.

If you don't have your own horse or pony and can only afford riding lessons, don't despair – many riding schools offer the chance to work towards various tests to encourage you to improve your riding and stable management.

The ABRS Tests for Weekly Riders (tests 0–10) are designed to encourage all riding school clientele, young and old alike, to gain a wider knowledge of the riding and care of horses. The Weekly Rider Alternative Flatwork Tests are a good choice for those who do not wish to jump. The Stable Management Tests, also graded from 0 to 10, are designed to provide nationally recognised standards of competence in the care and management of horses. If you take both the riding and stable management tests and pass test 9, you will qualify for the ABRS Bronze Award. Test 10 qualifies you for the Silver Award, then you are eligible to take the test for the Gold Award.

Many of the BHS approved riding schools offer their riders the opportunity to sit the BHS Progressive Riding Tests grades 1 to 12. The more riding and management tests you can take before leaving school, the better prepared you will be for working in the industry. Not only will you improve your knowledge, but also your confidence. Finally, if you can, take a recognised course in first aid such as those offered by the St John Ambulance or Red Cross.

If you have a choice of riding schools, try each one in turn and assess the following:

- Cost of lessons – is free tuition offered in return for helping?
- Additional lectures, and opportunities for taking examinations.
- Condition and temperament of the horses and ponies.
- Attitude and efficiency of the staff.
- Teaching skills and personalities of the instructors.
- Standard of stable management and riding technique – you won't learn high standards if they are not practised at the school!

Schoolwork

Now is the time to decide what would be the best option as a second string to your bow. The market for horse-associated activities is growing fast as more and more people take up horse riding as a hobby, career or business. Do you have a talent for writing? Are you good at arithmetic for accounting and book-keeping? Are you a good communicator and would feel at ease selling horse-associated products, or are you naturally good at art, making you creative enough to go into advertising or graphic design? Ask your teachers; they see best what latent talent you may have. You may not be using what you've got to its full potential at the moment because you're too busy reading a pony magazine behind your text book! Make the most of your education – while at school, learning is free!

Exams

Exam passes are essential in any industry; with such high unemployment, you will have a lot of competition for jobs, particularly the prestigious ones, so the more exam passes you have under your belt, the better it looks to an employer. The subjects most important for grooms and instructors are English, biology and maths.

English is important because you must be articulate when dealing with people. Good spelling and grammar are essential when applying for a job. You must be able to put your knowledge on paper and have legible handwriting, most exams in the industry involve written tests.

A study of *biology* will make exam revision easier when you have to study horse anatomy, diet and stud management. Finally, *mathematics* is important when stock-taking, ordering supplies, calculating bills and taking money from the public for services. In the long-term, if you aspire to run your own business, it would also be wise to take a course in book-keeping and accounting. You have to pay dearly in both time and money for such courses when you leave school!

Projects

Does your school run project-based exams? Choose a project that will help you learn and improve on skills you will need in the horse industry, such as horse business management for a maths project, or stable construction for technical drawing. Make a point of including these projects on your CV (curriculum vitae), the record of qualifications, skills and experience you have achieved during your working life.

A very shy, withdrawn person could be at a disadvantage when working with horses. Outgoing, friendly, and self-confident people who stand up for themselves may get on better. Does your school have a drama class? The skills learnt in drama, having to perform in front of an audience, will boost your confidence and help you to express your views. You really have to be able to stick up for yourself in life – this applies to working in any industry!

Physical education is another worthwhile subject. Working with horses requires you to be fit, and taking part in other sports will not only help you physically but will sharpen your mind and increase your confidence when in competition.

What you want to do in the horse world after you give up working with horses should determine what other exams and training you go for. If you want to go on to veterinary work, running your own business or strike out in a completely new direction, then you should think carefully about the qualifications you will need. The decision whether to stay on at school is entirely yours. I have no doubt you are restless to leave school and start your career, but it is well worth staying on an extra year or two at school or college, particularly if you want a job that requires a lot of academic qualifications. Aim high – you are only limited by your own ambition!

The importance of a good career plan cannot be stressed enough. Riding can be a high risk sport, and even if you don't think that you will tire of working with horses, physical injury could end your career at any time. Whether you succeed in the horse industry and achieve your desired goal is entirely up to you. Coming from a modest, unhorsey background isn't a problem. If you're ambitious and hard working you'll succeed, like Kath Connor BHSAI, who is twenty-five years old, and now works as a stable manageress:

> 'I started riding seriously when I was sixteen and went to train for my BHSAI at a riding centre in Scotland. With no tuition of any kind before that, I really was starting from scratch. I had no real career plan in mind, I just wanted to work in as many types of yards as possible to gain experience and take it from there.
>
> 'The training was all right and I enjoyed it, but I didn't learn as much during my training as I did through practical application. Reading about something takes a lot longer to sink in – you learn best by experience.
>
> 'After passing my AI, I was promoted to head girl. I stayed at the centre for two years helping to train new students and teaching the general public. Then I went to a disastrous job in Aberdeen, where the pay was dismal. At the interview I was told I could compete with my own horse every weekend – I got to one competition during the time I was there. I had to get up at five every morning to muck out thirty horses before my boss left, help her get her horses ready, see her off, then stay at home and get on with the other jobs.
>
> 'Out of stubborn pride, I stuck the job for eight months. At the time, I felt I would be a failure if I didn't give it a go. After that, I went home, totally depressed and never wanting to see another horse for as long as I lived!
>
> 'However, after a few weeks' rest, I went to work as an instructor for an Irish woman at a riding school in Scotland. That again was very hard work and the wage wasn't much better, but I wouldn't have swapped it for the world, I learned so much from her. She didn't do anything the BHS way – all her methods were totally unorthodox – but she always got results. Everyone there worked very hard. We started at six o'clock and we were lucky if we had finished by eight o'clock at night. My boss was a very hard worker, and she expected everyone else to be. I really respect her for that. I learnt a lot from her and loved every bit of my work, but in the end I was totally exhausted and on the verge of a nervous breakdown. I had to leave, I couldn't have done another stroke of work. We mutually agreed that it was time I moved on.

'After leaving the riding school, I worked temporarily at a trekking centre for the usual average wage but this time I got my horse's keep free. I was only there for the summer months, during which time my boss helped me find a very good job with the Swiss rider, Christine Gitzelman-Husband, who was based with event rider Polly Lochore in Scotland. I rode Christine's horses a lot, and helped school and jump them. Although I didn't get to compete on them, I was able to take my own horse round the local shows. I had the opportunity to go to Switzerland, but at the time I didn't want to sell my own horse. Animals are a big tie; I wouldn't advise you to have your own when you are working with horses as well.

'My wages improved substantially! I learnt a lot there, particularly how to look after three-day event horses, which I'd never done before. That was when I started thinking it was worth carrying on, because I was starting to get decent pay and learning a lot from travelling to big competitions.

'Shortly after my boss went back to Switzerland, a friend of mine asked me to go to London to look after her while she was convalescing from a back operation. I sold my horse and stayed in London for four months; I didn't enjoy city life, but I didn't miss horses either. However, horses are in the blood; I don't think you can ever get them out of your system. One spring morning I was walking down the road, when two police horses came clip-clopping round the corner. The scene looked so peaceful and natural! That day I started looking in *Horse and Hound* for jobs. I went for about six or seven interviews. At every single interview they said, "Yes, when can you start? Tomorrow?" I didn't find one that I really liked. It was by word of mouth that I heard about this, my current job, and was advised that it would be well worth my time. I phoned contacts asking what these people were like and everyone said go for it.

'I was interviewed very thoroughly. They asked for references – nobody else had. They wanted to know what I had done with my career, what I intended to do, what sort of training I had. They wanted to know everything about me. To me that sounded like a real job. Not somebody who says, "Start tomorrow, I don't care what you've done or want to do with your life."

'Elizabeth and Henry didn't. They wanted to see me ride, jump, do various jobs with the horses. I was here for about three hours with them testing and pushing me. I thought straight away, "This is the job I want!" It took a week for them to decide. They had a lot of other people to interview and were not going to take the first person who came along. When I phoned to ask if they'd made a decision, Elizabeth said, "We've got references from a few of your bosses and we've decided to employ you."

'I was so delighted, but as it happened, I had promised my former boss Christine, that when she got back to the UK I would do her horses for a couple of months. At the time I thought I would still be in London. I couldn't go back on my word to Chris, but Elizabeth and Henry were willing to wait because my references were so good. They got someone temporary until I could start, which was gratifying. I went back to Christine, who was now based in Waterstock, which is a very famous event yard in Oxfordshire, run by Lars Sederholm. I rode some excellent horses there and got lessons from Lars. Those two months were a great experience!

'Working for Elizabeth and Henry is excellent. They expect the best, but they give the best. All they are worried about is if I'm comfortable in the house, and that I'm happy with my job. If I have any problems, I can go to them; I don't have to suffer in silence. There are some people who work with horses but don't come up to scratch. I work really hard in this job, put my heart into it. My bosses know that and give me as good in return.

'My position here is yard manageress. I have only one person under me, but I literally do run the place. On top of a substantial wage, my bosses pay my electricity, phone rental, council tax, my competition entries, my BHS and BSJA memberships and all my travel expenses including food and accommodation – always the best hotels! I don't pay rent on the house and I get free use of a car and petrol. Working it out, my wages are probably double the cash I'm given, but if it wasn't for these perks it would be difficult to get by.

'My hours aren't long, 7.45 am to 4.45 pm, but I do work hard to maintain my standards. I get a day off a week plus an extra day a month, I also get bank holidays off (rare with horse work) and three weeks' paid holiday a year.

'On the competition side I'm very lucky. In the past I've had to pay for my own horse's entry fees and my membership fees. Elizabeth and Henry have given me what I call my own horse. They have nothing to do with her. I broke her in as a three-year-old, turned her away for the winter and brought her back in spring. She's jumping really well. I enter her for a lot of competitions; my bosses not only pay for the entries, but also for me to go on training courses.

They no longer compete themselves, so they fund me to go all over the country. Whatever I want to do with her, I can. They pay for the lot but I get her name and their name into *Horse and Hound* and that's good enough for them. I love the competition life. It does get a bit hectic at times because it's not all I do. If all I did was compete, it would be fine, but I've got to come back at the end of the day and do other things as well; say for foaling, I'll be up all night!

'Going back over my career, being older and wiser, I would certainly change the hours I had to work, knowing that really I didn't have to do it. In the beginning, I was so desperate to prove myself, I'd do anything, like being put on dangerous horses. I won't take risks any more; I have more self-esteem.

'For someone starting out, I would advise them not to take any rubbish from anybody. You don't have to – there are better jobs round the corner if you're patient. Don't just take the first one that comes along – I've made that mistake. The sooner people realise they don't have to accept poor pay, the better. Then employers will start appreciating the work grooms do and wages will rise.

'I hate the word "groom"; it doesn't reflect the importance of the job at all. Hippologist or equinologist sounds better! You've got to have a sense of humour in the horse world; if you don't laugh, you'll cry. I'm glad I chose to work with horses, I certainly don't regret it. I've been in the industry for nine years and I'm still enjoying it – you don't hear many people say they enjoy their job. Most people dread going to work in the mornings; I love it.'

Kath succeeded through hard work, a talent for riding and perseverance. Her periods of disillusionment after a stressful job, as a result of overwork or a bad employer, are not uncommon. It happens in a lot of jobs, not just with horses, and particularly when you are under great physical or mental strain. Take a rest, perhaps do a year at college to brush up on the skills you will require for your long-term aims but don't give up, keep working towards your objectives. Even if a job is not brilliantly paid or they won't let you compete, it's no reason to work to poor standards. At the end of the day, if you get a good reference it will have been well worth it! A previous employer that speaks very highly of you is worth far more than any qualification! Kath wasn't just employed because she was up to BHSAI standard; she was employed because she had proved herself hardworking, conscientious and reliable.

Chapter 2

Riding Instructors and Grooms

RIDING INSTRUCTORS

Once qualified as an instructor, you will play a very important role in setting the standard for tomorrow's horse owners and riders. Instructors spend most of their time teaching others. When working in a riding school, you must accept that your own riding opportunities will take second place to instructing. If you possess a true desire to teach, then this vocation will provide you with constant challenges and job satisfaction.

Over the centuries, the riding instructor's art has played a major part in the development of horsemanship for work and leisure. However, the qualities you need to be a successful instructor include more than just a certificate under your belt.

The difference between a mediocre instructor and an outstanding one is the ability to combine knowledge, a liking for all types of people plus a real talent for instructing. You should also be enthusiastic, self-confident and patient, with the ability to inspire the same qualities in your pupils. To keep your students' interest, you need to be articulate and entertaining and, above all, show a sense of humour. People ride for pleasure as well as improvement, and jollity is a wonderful remedy for nerves – but laugh with your pupils, not at them.

The people you will be expected to teach range from experienced riders, determined to improve their abilities, to mischievous children, whose attention spans won't exceed thirty seconds. You must be sufficiently adaptable to train the former with a dose of entertainment, and amuse the latter with a measure of instruction.

You will have to teach all manner of people in all weather conditions. Nothing is more miserable than a lesson on a cold, rainy day where the horses plod round like slaves on a treadmill and the riders sit like sacks of potatoes. You must be capable of livening-up the lesson to raise the spirits and improve the morale of both horses and riders.

Communication skills

You need to be articulate in order to explain clearly what is required of your pupils. A too quiet or squeaky voice can be a disadvantage when teaching. Good voice projection is invaluable, if you want to be heard without resorting to shouting; pupils will switch off if they cannot hear your instructions or they feel they are being yelled at. It may be that you have to compete with passing traffic noises, howling winds or the instructor teaching a group next to you.

Improvisation is an important asset for instructors, which is why some training centres include drama classes in their curriculum. Drama classes are a great way of building self-confidence and learning to think on your feet. As an instructor, you will have to stand up in front of an audience (your pupils) and perform. Unlike actors, however, you will not have a script, and you will have to rely on your powers of perception, equestrian skills and knowledge of the human psyche to get the best from your pupils. The instructor who stands in the middle of the school issuing commands to 'walk on, trot on, heels down and heads up' in a monotonous voice, is not going to inspire his pupils or encourage learning. You really have to weigh up the class and gear the lesson towards the needs and abilities of your pupils.

It's important that you not only make the lesson enjoyable for your pupils, but that you also improve their riding and inspire them to persevere and return to you for more lessons. The instructor must be able to plan a balanced lesson in which the pupils progress and also plan a whole series of lessons which set targets and ultimately achieve them. The mark of good instructors, either freelance or at riding schools, is the loyalty shown by their pupils who stay with them for as long as they can afford.

Chief instructor at the TM International School of Horsemanship, Mary Tyrell qualified in physical education before going to Nigeria as a PE teacher with Voluntary Services Overseas. She then went to Norway:

> 'I've ridden since I was a child, on and off, and while I was in Norway, I worked for an international institution, coping with immigrant and refugee children. It was set up on a farm, and gradually the work involved animals, including horses. I then qualified as a social worker and also got more involved with the

horses, so I trained and qualified in Norway as an instructor. It was there I met my husband, Ted, and together we set up a riding school in Norway. After a few years we moved back to England, taking the horses with us, and set up this school about five years ago.

'The Norwegian riding instructor's qualification I have is, I suppose, the equivalent of a BHS Stage IV in Britain, as the Norwegians have a very similar system. The PE training I did initially helps me a lot as an instructor because I look at the person's body and "conformation" a lot more than a riding instructor normally would. You tend to get a lot of emphasis put on how the horse is going, and not so much training in how the person is reacting.

'I think if you're just instructing and not receiving instruction yourself, you tend to get very set in your ways. Getting instruction yourself will inspire your own teaching and you might get a slightly different view on how to correct something, which puts that little bit of spark into the lesson. For someone who wants to make a career as an instructor, you've got to be quite patient, have an outgoing personality and a certain amount of riding ability yourself so you can understand what you are trying to do with the horse.

'You've got to absorb a lot from the people you are with and take them into consideration a great deal. I think there's too much concentration at times on the horse at the riding school level, and you should give a little more attention to the rider. Of course, as you get higher up, the rider himself is thinking of how the horse is going.

'I think at riding school level you've got to be far more of a teacher than an instructor, and make it so that it's not just fun for the sake of keeping the customer happy but also that you show improvement in the customer so they understand that what they are doing is in order to make life better for the horse. Eventually when they get their own horse, they will hopefully follow on in that way. You've also got to be quite strong – it's a hard physical job; you don't just get to stand and teach, although that can be quite wearing in itself.'

The school trains both British and foreign students and Mary is responsible for recruiting:

'For obvious reasons, it's difficult to interview foreign students but I interview the British ones. From a riding point of view, it doesn't really matter what level they are as long as they are prepared to take instruction, then we can improve them anyway. When assessing a

> student, it's just a matter of judging how long it would take to get them up to standard. Personality wise, you can't tell too much at an interview about a person's character. We normally take trainees on trial and we soon find out what they are capable of. If they are a very nervous, withdrawn type of person, then we know they are not going to do very well.'

As chief instructor, Mary's routine also involves supervision of the yard:

> 'I'm usually on the yard about 7 am, feeding and supervising the morning routine of mucking out, catching ponies for lessons and grooming. After breakfast, I'm instructing or giving theory lessons for the rest of the day, at the same time checking that staff and trainees are doing their particular tasks to contribute to the smooth running and management of the yard. If you've given out responsibilities, it's your job to check that they are done correctly.
>
> 'With regard to riding, a lot of young people don't realise that when they take on the responsibility of instructing at a riding school, they won't have nearly so much time to ride. It's not so bad if you are in a yard with an indoor school as you can ride late in the evening, and of course you can ride outside on summer evenings. But you must be prepared to accept that your riding will take second place to instructing.'

Freelance Instructor/Trainer

Going 'freelance' seems to be the ambition of many would-be instructors, but few will have seriously considered the implications. A riding school will already have regular numbers of pupils each week; as a freelance, you will have to build up your list of clients from scratch. Unless they have horses of their own, you will not be able to take on pupils from the school where you trained. Your clients must have their own horses and their own facilities. Unfortunately, many people who own horses do not have the money to take instruction as well, although most realise that they are not beyond teaching.

Although you may be well qualified, this does not mean people will come hammering at your door; you will have to earn yourself a good reputation and build up your list of clients gradually. You can offer services such as clipping and trimming but you will need to invest in a good pair of clippers, which are expensive to buy and costly to run, so your number of clients will have to be quite high. All this takes time, so you must have some other means of living until you are earning enough to support yourself. As a freelance instructor, you will be working as a self-employed person, more details of which can be found in Chapter Seven – Self-Employment.

Equestrian Tourism and Leisure

Tourists and leisure riders provide a large slice of financial income for riding schools and trekking centres, and there are considerable employment opportunities stemming from the popularity of riding holidays. Today, employers are looking not only for staff who are good with horses but also those who really enjoy being with people, especially children, so that the clients will feel welcome and enjoy their holiday or trek all the more. Training opportunities for tourism and leisure are now well catered for with the introduction of the BHS Equestrian Tourism exams, (see Chapter Eight – Training for more information).

Working in a riding school will also involve taking hacks. Many of the people who go trekking may not be interested in serious riding, therefore your job will be to escort the ride and see that the clients enjoy themselves, ride safely and with consideration for others. Most people are pretty sensible, but you will always get the odd one or two who try to show off, so you must stay firmly in control but not be so strict as to spoil their enjoyment of the ride.

Some clients are extremely nervous when they are riding for the first time, particularly across open country, so you must be capable of assuring them and taking their mind off their fears. Conversation is a good way of distracting their fear and building confidence. The horses and ponies used in most trekking centres usually have kind, accommodating natures and are well capable of looking after the people in their care.

If you are taking out a large party of people of whom you have no previous knowledge, you must be capable of assessing their weight, confidence and abilities and allocating them suitable horses. Your daily routine in a riding holiday or trekking centre will include the care of both stabled and grass-kept horses and ponies, including catching them and grooming. Once the morning chores are done, the rest of the day is spent tacking and untacking horses for rides and lessons and escorting rides. There is a lot more to working in and running a riding centre for tourists than you may at first think. It's certainly a lot of fun, particularly if you like working with people as much as horses. It can be a well-paid job and there are also some very good opportunities for work overseas, such as summer camps in America and in European riding centres which cater for British tourists.

Opportunities for Grooms

The Professional Groom

Most youngsters start out in the horse industry because they want to work with horses. Grooms have a reputation for being under-paid, over-worked and even exploited. While this is true for some, it is not always the case. If you lack ambition, initiative and motivation, then you may end up working in a dead-end job for little pay but if you are hard-working, skilled and motivated then you will have the confidence to go for the better jobs.

However, it cuts both ways. As I have said before, good grooms are like gold dust. Someone with a vacancy that offers good pay and accommodation, as well as all the extra perks such as household bills paid, use of car etc., can rightly expect an employee to be hard-working, loyal, skilled and responsible. Such employees are hard to find.

It takes a special kind of person to be a professional groom. The first thing to consider is, are you physically capable?

'It's a fairly physical job,' explains show jumper David Broome, 'so you need to be healthy and strong to do the work. It's no good having a dainty, dinky thing that couldn't push a decent wheelbarrow!'

Contrary to popular belief, you also have to be fairly bright if you want to get the best jobs.

'Things can happen in a professional yard that you need somebody with a brain to sort out – on the spot!' explains David. 'Horses can get up to all sorts of tricks; if somebody is dim and doesn't think, then you have accidents.'

Training

The qualifications needed to become a groom are not necessarily achieved by sitting exams. The general consensus among employers and employees in the industry is that, if you have ridden, and in particular competed a lot as a youngster, then you will probably have enough knowledge and confidence to go straight into groom's work. However, I feel that having some sort of professional qualification helps you realise your full potential and will discourage you from taking jobs that offer pay and conditions beneath the standard you should set yourself. Qualifications are also useful in making employers realise that you are a professional and your wages, work and living conditions should reflect that status.

If you feel that your riding and equestrian knowledge is limited (perhaps you have not had much direct contact with horses) then why not try the various exams on offer, such as the BHS Competition Groom's exam, where you will be working for a recognised BHS approved trainer in a competition yard, learning all the requirements to that trainer's satisfaction then taking the exam at a BHS exam centre. The Competition Groom's exam has the option of being in a riding or non-riding capacity. The NPS Groom's Diploma, run on similar lines, will provide an excellent basis on which to train as a stud groom.

It must be said, however, that once you have passed these exams, you will still have an awful lot to learn. Every yard in the industry has its own way of doing things, and that way may not necessarily be by the book. For example, the training and fitness programme of a show jumper is very different to that of a racehorse. You will have to be prepared to follow 'house rules'.

The beauty of working in professional yards is that you have the opportunity to learn many different ways of doing things, and in some cases, how not to do things! This is the best way to learn. When you are an employer yourself, you will have a lot of knowledge and experience to call on.

In competition, racing or hunting yards, most professional grooms have to master the art of plaiting up a horse within ten to fifteen minutes; can you? Being so efficient that you can work without supervision is also of paramount importance. David Broome likes to be sure that his horses are being well looked after while he is away, so it's important for him to have reliable and conscientious staff:

'I expect high standards from my staff. Horses to be well looked after, fed regularly, yard kept tidy, gates shut, that sort of thing,' he maintains. 'In return, my responsibilities towards my staff are to see that not only are their living conditions as good as I can make them, but also their working conditions. I think it's important that they've got nice horses to look after. There's a lot more pleasure in looking after a good horse than there is in looking after a useless one. It shouldn't be so, but if I was doing their job, I would rather look after a decent horse.'

Having successful horses to look after compensates for not being able to compete yourself:

'It's nice to work for somebody who wins. When they win, in a sense you win as well. We all get a buzz when the horses do well,' explains David's head groom, Emma Storey.

When looking for work as a groom, there are certain points to take into account. Do you want to compete yourself? Many people are not interested in the competitive side of riding, but take pride and pleasure in looking after horses that compete successfully with professional riders. The riding aspect of groom's work, in this instance, primarily involves exercising horses to get them fit for their work.

Initially, fitness programmes involve a lot of road work. As horses get fitter, they get stronger and fresher. You have to be calm and effective to keep control of them in traffic, and keep to the required pace when you are doing canter work. When you start off as a groom, you will begin by riding the quieter, easier horses and progress to the more difficult ones. You will get help with your riding, but you must show some ability.

'I'll help the grooms with their riding to an extent,' explains David. 'There's no point in letting a groom ride badly. But,' he adds, 'if they're totally useless on a horse, there's not much point them being in the job.'

Apart from the head groom, Emma, who will work the horses while he is away, the grooms in David's yard never jump the horses. This is not always the case. In some yards, it may be that there is a lot of dealing and training of young horses, and often grooms will get the opportunity to jump, with the main rider acting as coach assessing the horse's progress. You may even get a chance to compete. However, because competition riders are away so much, the person you are most likely to learn from in any yard is the head groom. How much you absorb will depend on whether you are willing to learn, as head girl Emma Storey points out:

> 'When youngsters first come here I don't expect them to be able to pull manes, clip, or turn out to the standard I would want them to. If they stay here long enough, I'm always willing to teach them. If they want to learn, that's good; I'm only too happy to show them how to clip and all the other useful skills. When you come into a yard, you start at the bottom of the ladder. But over the years you learn to ride really well because you end up sitting on all types of horses.
>
> 'I do like to have staff that stay. It's better for the horses if you've got people that want to stay in a job rather than people coming and going. We had one girl who'd been here for five years, but has just

> left. She decided to get out of the horse industry, which many grooms do after so long. Sometimes they get married, or go abroad or some just want a change of direction. To be a successful groom you've got to be able to ride well, be very patient and be willing to put in a long day sometimes.'

When you are a groom for a successful rider, often you won't compete yourself. Event rider Mary Thomson explains why:

> 'My grooms don't get the opportunity to compete, but that's a stipulation I make before anybody comes to my yard because the horses are privately owned. My sponsor pays for me to ride for her, so there isn't the chance for anybody to event any of the horses. It's just the way it is.
>
> 'The job of groom is ideal for somebody like my groom, Annie, who adores the horses, but isn't brave enough to compete herself. She gets her kick out of watching the horses she looks after being successful.'

However, if you do want to compete yourself one day, working short-term for a successful competitor can be useful.

> 'If anybody is competitive, it's okay for them to come to my sort of yard for say, six months, see how things should be done and travel to events. But six months is enough, if you want to compete; it all depends on how good a rider you are and how much money you've got. Before you start to compete, however, go and work in a yard. Okay, if possible, my sort of yard for a short time, but then try to get into a yard where you can ride. If it wasn't for the two-and-a-half years I did in Sheila Wilcox's dealing yard, there's no way I'd be where I am now. That job involved riding many different horses. My horses can be deceptively easy for people to ride because they're all well trained and lovely natured. Some people think they can ride, then they're stuck on a young horse that bucks and turns itself inside out and they don't know what to do. If you want to go on to compete, you really need to learn by riding the bad ones as well the good to experience all the awful things that horses can do. You'll learn how to correct those mistakes and get them going well.'

For grooms who don't want to ride at all, the best opportunities can be found on stud farms, where you can concentrate on building up a career in stud management and stable husbandry. Working in the racing industry (see Chapter Four for more details) provides excellent scope for learning high standards in stud work and professional grooming. Thoroughbred breeding plays a large part in the industry and has its own training programmes for stud management and stable husbandry. If you prefer travelling to riding, then there are openings for travelling grooms in both the Thoroughbred and non-Thoroughbred industries.

As in all careers, you may not find the right position straight away. Apart from the job itself, the people you work for, and with, are equally important. Having an understanding and caring employer goes a long way towards job satisfaction.

Before she started competing for a living, Mary Thomson was an employee herself, and because of her experience, is more sympathetic towards her own staff:

> 'When I was in a dealing yard for two-and-a-half years it was such hard work! I had a tough time there and I always thought that if I ever got to the position of employing someone, I would jolly well make sure that they had a really nice time!
>
> 'You've got to think how they feel. Working with the horses is fairly monotonous with the daily grind of mucking out and grooming, etc. But that's one of the things you've got to realise; it's not as glamorous as it looks from the outside.
>
> 'It's also important to make sure your staff work reasonable hours – although when you're competing that can go right up the creek! Generally, I try to look after my staff, not work them too much and be friendly with them. It's very important to make sure you talk to each other all the time and air your views.'

Employer David Broome also understands the importance of liaising with his staff:

> 'You need a happy yard. Happy grooms mean happy horses – then you are successful. If you have an upset yard and go to a show, no one speaks to each other and the atmosphere is terrible, so you never win anything. I do see it happen; it's absolutely useless! Any antagonism in a yard is immediately picked up by the horses and affects their performance. That's why I look after my staff, because I like my horses to be looked after as best I can.'

Finding Employment as a Groom

Wages

One of the most important conditions of employment is the rate you will be paid. The horse industry is notorious for poor wages, but is it fact, or simply reputation?

The average wage when starting out with horses, for example, working in a riding school or for a private employer, is usually below the minimum earnings required to pay National Insurance contributions. (By qualifying for National Insurance contributions you will be entitled to sickness or unemployment benefit should you ever have to stop work. The contribution is revised in the Budget each year and your local tax office can tell you what the current amount is.) The keep of your own horse should also be taken into consideration. If you were being paid just below that minimum level, provided with accommodation but had to buy your own food, pay household bills and your horse's keep, then you are not getting a fair deal!

If you are offered just below the minimum wage but with full board included, remember that you still have riding clothes and equipment to buy. (You'll wear out a lot of clothes working with horses.) Toiletries, washing powder, travel expenses on your day off, the birthday card you need to buy for your mum – all these will soon make your cash disappear. Unless you are being offered the chance to compete, all expenses paid, or you are being given riding instruction from a professional, don't accept such a wage, even with no experience under your belt!

The best guide is to accept a wage that is high enough to qualify you for National Insurance contributions plus board and lodging on top; the keep of your horse would be an added bonus but in fairness to your employer, they are losing money on the time you spend with your own horse during working hours.

Many employers in the horse industry offer similar wages to those set in the agricultural industry, which is a good solution provided you have accommodation included, as most agricultural workers do, usually in the form of a tied cottage or flat.

As you get more experienced and build up a reputation for being professional in your work, you will find that you get the better-paid jobs, usually as a professional rider's groom or in successful commercial yards, where you are expected to earn every penny. In this situation, your wage should reflect the level of responsibility you are given.

Accommodation (but not necessarily meals) should be included.

Work out a budget; you should have enough money left to buy clothes, save up for holidays and go out with your friends. This may not sound much, but if your job also provides a house or flat and the use of a car, then you are much better off than the average secretary or shop worker with a weekly net pay. With no added perks such as accommodation included, they have to pay the rent, buy food, pay the bills, buy toiletries, as well as pay car running costs or bus fares to and from their place of work. Today's high cost of living usually doesn't leave anything over for clothes, socialising and saving unless they take on extra work or are helped out by parents or a partner. Counting up the perks, in some jobs, you will have a substantial additional hidden wage! It can be argued that at least a secretary or shop worker has to work fewer hours per day, in a less physically demanding job and has free weekends. What these jobs lack in physical stress they make up for in mental stress, and these days, a lot more demands for unpaid overtime are made because employers cannot afford extra staff. When it comes to other types of job, the grass isn't necessarily greener on the other side.

Many people who work in shops, factories or offices might say, 'I hate being stuck indoors with the nine to five grind – I'd love to work with horses, but you don't get paid much, do you?' Unless you are in the horse industry, the fringe benefits are little known. Wages for grooms will never be brilliant and don't usually go much higher unless you are a chief instructor or in another managerial position. Working with horses will always be a labour of love – no one ever does it just for the money.

Accommodation

Most jobs with horses will include some sort of accommodation.

Live-in as family means you will be staying in the home of your employer. For this situation to work, you must be able to get on with other people, and possibly not mind having their children about. In this situation, you'll obviously need to like children; if you don't, then avoid 'live-in as family' jobs and those that say 'some baby-sitting involved'. Also, your employer should not be so superior that you feel uncomfortable in their home.

Self-contained flat is usually within the house of your employer but with your own bedroom, bathroom, living room and kitchen. Be cautious when considering a job with live-in accommodation – you may end up doing housework, dog walking, and if they have children, nannying and babysitting. That's fair enough – if it's made clear to you that the job will involve such duties and your wages reflect the extra work, and it may be that you only have one or two horses to look after.

Cottage, flat or caravan adjacent to stables. This type of accommodation has its advantages and disadvantages. Having your job situated outside your front door is great for those who hate getting up in the mornings; it means you don't have to allow time to get to work. Also you can have lunch at home, so you don't have to bother with sandwiches or the expense of eating out. If it's described as shared accommodation, it's also important to be able to get on with other people.

The disadvantages include never really getting away from your work. You might even be expected to act as a security guard and check the horses throughout the evening. One employer, paranoid about being burgled, wouldn't let her groom off the premises if she was going away and was constantly phoning to check that she hadn't gone out for the evening. Needless to say she didn't stipulate that condition in the interview! It's reasonable to be asked to do night stables or evening feeds on a rota system when you live in, but you are entitled to your own life and not accountable to your employer for your every move.

Accommodation provided close to where you work is probably the ideal situation. You're not on the employer's doorstep so if you want a night out, or have relatives and friends to stay then you don't have to worry about asking permission, or listening to reprimands about your social activities. Accommodation is usually furnished. Standards can vary, but in any case, it is up to you to show consideration by not abusing the facilities provided.

Live out means finding your own accommodation which should be reasonably close to your place of work or, if you're lucky, you can live with your parents or partner. If you do live out, then expect a higher rate of pay because you will have more outgoings every month. If you live at home, you shouldn't expect your parents to cover all living expenses.

Hours worked and time off

It is impossible to lay down the exact hours worked when it comes to a groom's average working week; competitions, travel, sick horses, visiting vets or blacksmiths and clients can put paid to your lunch hours and free evenings. The average working day is between eight and ten hours, but during the competition season it can be up to eighteen hours! Not all of this time is hard labour; you could be travelling to a show for four hours and the work you do when you arrive may be intense but brief, leaving you time to wander around and enjoy the day's events.

Competitions are usually held at weekends and bank holidays, so if you cherish your weekends being free to shop and socialise, then think twice before working as a groom. A day off is usually taken during the week, and it's not always possible to take one every week. However, a good employer will try to ensure that their grooms have a long weekend off once a month during the busiest times. It is lack of time off that contributes to grooms becoming physically run down so quickly, a fact that is often overlooked by many employers.

Many people who work with horses are dedicated to the job and throw themselves into their work. But it is important to realise that there is more to life than horses. Making time for a social life and relationships is important for morale, as event groom Annie Collings has learnt:

> 'Socially, I'm very lucky in that I was brought up here and have a lot of my old school friends to go out with. It's okay now while we're quiet, but when the show season starts, I'm away most weekends. You can't be so party-minded then; if you've got a four o'clock start, you don't want to be out till one or two in the morning. It has been done, but I suffer! It's not a good idea, especially if I've got to help drive as well – you've got to have your wits about you when getting horses ready for travelling. My social life goes a bit up and down during the event season and I don't really have much time for relationships; they seem to go out the door rapidly. Boyfriends can't understand why I'm up here all the time.
>
> 'In my job I love the travelling, I love the horses, but you feel sometimes that life's passing you by. When I look around and see how all my friends are married, and a lot of them have children, I keep thinking I'm getting old at twenty-seven. Everybody else says, "Don't worry, you've plenty of years ahead of you yet!"
>
> 'I'd be quite happy to stay here indefinitely, but I know there must be more to life than this. If you'd asked me two years ago, I would have said that I didn't want anything else. But you change and your perception of what you want in life changes. I'd like the time to have a serious relationship, maybe even have children one day.
>
> 'Mary [Thomson] is a brilliant boss, but she has a very good boyfriend and she can come home and go out with him. When I come back, although I have a lot of friends I can ring up and go out with, it's not the same, is it? You get so blinkered in this lifestyle. There's a lot of travelling, a lot of parties and things but you've got to think of your future as well.'

Holidays and holiday pay

When it comes to holidays, time off and wages, a lot depends on the success and generosity of your employer. Competition grooms do not have a statutory pay scheme and are not protected by associations, unions or laws. This lack of protection can make you vulnerable to exploitation, so it is important that you get a contract of employment and that both employer and employee are quite clear as to their obligations and duties.

In competition yards, you may find yourself laid off for a few months at the end of the season when the horses are out at grass. Event horses are usually roughed off from October to December and Annie Collings uses this period to recharge her batteries:

> 'The first couple of years I was kept in full-time work. While the horses were out at grass from October to December, there were plenty of odd jobs, like painting stables, that needed doing, and usually a couple of horses to ride. But in the last two years I have been laid off while the horses are resting. It's a good opportunity to catch up on rest and travel round the world, which I really enjoy. By Christmas, the horses start coming back in and I get back to work.'

This is the time that most professional grooms will use for rest and holidays, but remember, after your holiday pay runs out, you are technically unemployed and could be entitled to unemployment benefit if you have been paying National Insurance contributions. You may have the option of getting your job back next season or you may want to try for another job soon after you leave.

Holiday pay entitlements are based on the length of time you have worked for an employer. You should be entitled to one week's paid holiday for every three months you have worked full time. Jobs that don't involve you being laid off temporarily will usually give three to five weeks' paid holiday.

Choices

The aspect of groom's work you choose will depend on your own preferences. You may love the bravery of eventing, the glitter of show jumping or the style and intensity of dressage. Whatever area you choose, remember that a lot of hard work goes on behind the scenes and you will be the one doing it! As groom, you will play a very important part in the team. Horses are greatly affected by the competence and consideration of their grooms, so you need to build up a good relationship with the horses in your charge and always put their needs before your own.

To be a successful team member, you must have a real interest in what you do, and not just go along with anything for the sake of being around horses. Learning as much as you can about your particular role will provide a sound basis on which to develop your career. You should be able to perform all the duties required of a groom without having to be asked, and perform them well. Aim to make your mark in the industry.

Dealing Yards

In dealing yards you will be handling people as often as you will horses, so you will need a good sales pitch as well as scrupulous ethics. One bad deal can lose you a lot of potential customers. In this line of work you must be a very good rider because you will be schooling all sorts of horses. In particular, you may be working with the bad horses that have been bought cheaply, as your employer knows they might make a profit if their problems are corrected. The horse's problem may not be in riding him but instead he may have a stable vice or phobia, or as is often the case, excessive nervousness as a result of bad handling. You need to be firm but sympathetic towards the animals in your care, many of which will have been mistreated or spoilt.

Working as a groom in a dealing yard offers more in the way of good experience than good pay. It's hard work, long hours, average pay, but what you learn in this type of yard will provide a good basis on which to start your career.

Dressage

Dressage hasn't benefited from media coverage in the same way as other equestrian sports. Those who work and compete in this sport, keeping British riders in the top rankings, often go unrecognised. The general public may be familiar with names like Nick Skelton and Ian Stark, but they may not recognise Carl Hester or Richard Davison.

However, dressage is the fastest growing equestrian discipline in the UK. It combines dedicated training with immaculate presentation, and to succeed in dressage involves many hours of skill and patience. The road to the top is long, so you must love the sport for itself and not just the winning. There are many good riders in dressage, and the competition is close. The difference between winning or coming second can be a matter of a few points. To be successful is to be outstanding; you must ride with panache. German trainer, Herr Homrigh-Hausen, sums up the qualities of a successful team:

'Every horse is capable of being a dressage horse, and as his rider you must lift him out of the mundane and make him shine like a star! It is the same for riders: no-one is born to dressage; it takes many hours of training combined with an unyielding desire for perfection.'

A great deal of patience is needed in training, which may be why it has the reputation of being a rider's final option in equestrian sports.

'A lot of people come into dressage later on in life,' explains dressage rider Vanessa Cheffing, BHSII. 'I don't think it's because their nerve goes for jumping; it's simply that you find as you get older and a bit more patient, it becomes very interesting.'

To work with dressage horses, you must enjoy training, because that is what dressage is all about. You must also be able to turn out to a very high standard. Presentation is half the battle. If the horse and rider know they look good, they will perform better. You need a calm temperament to work with dressage horses; you cannot afford to upset them before a test. In fact, the same could be said of all competition horses.

Driving

As with dressage, interest in driving is growing rapidly. By joining the British Driving Society you will be entitled to take their proficiency tests in four grades, which provides not only proof of your driving ability but also, as the tests are based on the BHS Stages, you can adapt your skills to other areas of groom's work.

In a driving yard, your duties will include the art of preparing horses for the show ring; a coach-and-four or heavy horses pulling a dray at a show are still very popular and impressive sights. To get the horses and their harness up to show standards requires a lot of elbow grease and pride in your work. The opportunities for driving grooms are quite varied and you can find work that involves combined driving trials, coaching (private four-in-hand driving), or heavy horses (which are often sponsored by breweries).

Eventing

Eventing is the ultimate for discipline of both horse and rider. To train a horse to the level of fitness required to complete a gruelling cross-country circuit, but still keep it level-headed enough to perform a calm and collected dressage and show jumping test is no mean feat. To work as an eventing groom requires physical stamina and a sharp mind. High standards and a sense of responsibility are expected when you work for a successful rider, but job satisfaction is equally high. Annie Collings, who has been with eventer Mary Thomson for five years, agrees:

> 'If I'd just been in a riding or trekking centre, I don't think I would have lasted as long. I like routine and I like to be organised and know what's happening and when. I'm not worked too hard and I'm well paid for the job. I get £190 a week (gross), three weeks' paid holiday a year and free livery for my horse.
>
> 'Mary is a great boss, really good. She's easy-going to the extent that she'll understand if you have a problem, but she expects us to look tidy, the horses to be well groomed and tack to be cleaned. You can't take short cuts. I just have to get my head down and get on with it. For example, Mary likes the horses to be turned out for an hour every day, and you can't not turn them out to save extra work, because she'd know if they weren't.
>
> 'I'm quite happy with my job and I'm very fond of all the horses. I often wonder when I'll stop but I like to see the horses through their career, like Willie [King William], he's my baby. Taking him to the Olympics in Barcelona was excellent. It's not every day you get to the Olympics, although quite a few of the three days were party time. I went to the Europeans in Ireland the previous year, which we won. That too, was a good experience, and a lot of fun!'

As a groom, it is up to you to keep the horses happy and fit for the season and to do this you must have a lot of stable management knowledge and a real love for the horses in your care. Eventing is one of the few sports where amateurs can compete successfully against the professionals, so there are opportunities to work for lesser-known event riders, or in dealing yards where you may be offered the opportunity to compete yourself, or perhaps hunt if you are a good enough rider.

Hunting

Working with hunters is one of the toughest jobs you can do in the horse industry; it involves long hours and a lot of hard work. However, if you get a job that offers you the opportunity to hunt, then it can provide some of the best days of your life. Before working for Mary Thomson, Annie Collings spent two seasons working for a local hunt master in Devon:

> 'At the hunt stables I used to ride the Master's second horse quite a lot, which was great because I got a lot of hunting in those two years. I thoroughly enjoyed it and still go hunting with my own horse quite often. It's nice to get out and see all the local people I know. It's not great hunting around here, but the social side is fun. People are not at all competitive out hunting and everyone looks out for everyone else. It makes a nice change, for at work you're running to a schedule all the time, getting horses exercised and trying to get everything ready for an event.'

Looking after hunters is very hard work. When horses come home from a day's hunt, they are usually covered in mud from top to toe. Hunting is a winter sport and hosing horses down with cold water in cold weather dries and cracks the skin. You have to wait until the mud dries then brush off every last bit, and as it's not a job to be left until morning, you could be grooming hunters until ten o'clock at night. Horses are usually exhausted after a day's hunt and need the best of care and attention to keep them in good form. Initially, the riding side involves the usual fitness programme of three to five weeks' road work, then progressing to hill and canter work. Once the horses have hunted for a few weeks, the hunting alone is sufficient to keep them fit and your job will consist mainly of road work to keep them ticking over.

Starting your career in a hunt yard is a good way into the horse industry. Many top grooms have started their career in this way, including show jumping groom, Emma Storey:

> 'I've had no formal training in working with horses; I had my own horses until I was about eighteen or nineteen, then I left home and went to work with hunters at Hickstead for a year. We did a six-month hunting season, which was good fun. During the summer I helped with the shows and rode the young horses. Conditions were good – the pay wasn't – but my boss was very good to work for.'

Hunting generates many jobs within the horse industry. It provides full-time employment for around 13,000 people, and indirectly employment for another 27,000. To work in a hunt yard, as opposed to looking after the horses of someone who hunts as a hobby, is definitely a way of life for hunt grooms, or hunt servants, to use the correct term. Hunting is not for the faint-hearted – like all aspects of country life it's earthy and practical and there is little room for sentiment; even the best hunters end up as food for hounds. It's all to do with practical management and utilising resources.

Hunt staff can be very well looked after by the Master of Foxhounds in hunt kennels. This area of the industry often has openings for married couples, usually the husband will be employed for the kennel work, including the slaughter of horses and other animals as feed for the hounds, and the wife will look after and exercise the horses. Both may share the duties of hound exercise and whipping-in. Working in a hunt yard is hard work, but living and work conditions are usually high. Wages can vary, although you are well looked after in other respects.

Polo

Polo grooms are also dedicated horse people because of the long hours involved. The job involves a lot of travelling to matches as well as many hours of hanging around. Polo grooms are, in general, well looked after and often get the opportunity to travel internationally. There are many polo players who come onto the English circuit during the season and offer job opportunities in Australia, New Zealand and the Americas. Also, through your contacts with the people you work with in yards over here, you can get jobs overseas quite easily.

New Zealand rider Tim Keyte came to Britain last year and liked it so much, he decided to stay. Tim now runs a polo yard near Cirencester which offers livery for polo ponies, and with low- and medium-goal level Argentine and New Zealand Thoroughbreds of its own, the yard also offers polo lessons and chukkas for amateur riders of all ages and abilities. Tim explains that the work of the grooms in this type of yard is similar to riding school work, with the additional bonus of travelling to polo matches:

> 'Our girls don't start until eight o'clock unless we have a match at ten, then they start a bit earlier. Because we are a huge yard, we have one guy on the yard who does all the mucking out so the girls don't have to bother themselves with that. They just do the horses and look after the people who come and go. We always have people coming for lessons, so they're busy tacking and untacking horses most of the

> day. Several people who keep their horses here play at Cirencester Park during the summer and one of those will be playing most days, so somebody has to go to the park with those horses. Normally we try to finish about five o'clock. The grooms here get plenty of opportunities to ride, not only exercising but joining in chukkas to make up numbers if players let us down. Most, however, are content just to look after and love the horses.'

The working life of polo ponies, particularly those used for high-goal matches, is hard and fast and their grooms must be capable of taking good care of them both at home and at matches. This involves a lot of careful grooming and attention; you can't cut corners otherwise you will impair the performance of the ponies.

On the riding aspect, polo ponies are not so much highly strung as highly attuned. High-goal ponies are trained very much like racehorses, so you need to be able to keep a cool head to ride them. They are very sensitive to the aids and can break into a gallop, stop and turn on a sixpence at the slightest pressure. They have to be well behaved on the polo field, so in general, they are fairly good natured to exercise at home; you are more likely to be taken off with rather than thrown off, so you have to be a fairly relaxed and competent rider to keep control of them.

To be a polo rider, you don't have to have an immense amount of money to start with, but you do need talent and time to develop that talent. If you can already ride, that's definitely a plus, but not essential to start with. Because of the increase in popularity of polo, there are several schools which offer lessons and a chance to play in practice chukkas. Once you get a few lessons, depending on how you go, you can then start playing the practice chukkas which are played two or three times a week.

'If you want to play in proper matches, that's when it starts to get expensive,' explains Tim. 'First you have to join an affiliated club. For example, Cirencester's annual membership fee will cost you about £2,000. On top of that, you'd have the entry fee for your team, which could be as high as £400. If you need to hire horses, that will cost you probably about £40–£50 a chukka. Owning them is a lot more expensive. Right at the beginning you can probably get away with two horses to start with, if you only play once a week. If you start playing more than that, you'll need at least four.'

To play polo professionally requires hours of practice. You either need a large disposable income, or you need to possess the talent to get yourself on a team that is sponsored by a patron. Professionals are said to be only as good as their last three games and contracts last only for a season at a time. In most polo teams, one of the players is usually also the patron, putting up the money for the team in return for the kudos of playing.

The polo season in Britain starts around the end of April and lasts until October. However, polo is very much an international sport and if you are in a top team, you could find yourself travelling to matches across Europe and during the winter, to places such as Argentina or Palm Beach in Florida. It's not impossible to play polo for a living, but like all sporting professionals, you do need a lot of talent to get the financial backing.

Showing

Showing horses and ponies requires a great deal of patience and perfection. Success in the ring depends entirely upon the preferences of the judges and it's not unusual to be placed first at one show and last a week later at another. Showing is very popular among amateurs. The large numbers of entries at shows make showing, either as rider or groom, a very long and monotonous task.

On the professional side, showing is the shop window for the breed societies in Britain and the meticulous standards required in this discipline mean that you have to be very dedicated to the art. Show horses have to be brought up to a level of fitness where they look the part. For example, show hunters, in order to cope with the rigours of hunting, need a bit more meat on them than event horses or polo ponies. Horses and ponies are usually shown in hand up until the age of four then ridden under saddle. In working hunter classes horses are required to jump a round of fences of the type you would come across out hunting, such as stiles, water jumps and gates.

As a groom, you will be responsible for the exercise and day-to-day grooming of your charges. On the travelling side, you will have to pack, and be careful to remember all the right paraphernalia.

At the shows, you will assist the rider with preparation of the horses and be responsible for making sure they are tacked up and ready for your rider to switch over between classes, and possibly be responsible for collecting numbers from the show secretary. You need an unflappable disposition for this job, because you're efficiency affects the rider as much as the horse! Very often, opportunities for showing coincide with stud work, so you may find yourself doing both types of job.

Show Jumping

Show jumping is an international sport with extensive television coverage that proliferates a following of millions. Not surprisingly, many youngsters are attracted to the sport.

'In show jumping, there's a lot of hard work that goes on behind the glitter of the arena and when youngsters come into the sport there are a lot of angles they've probably never thought of,' warns show jumper David Broome. 'The hours involved are very unsociable. It's always weekend work when it comes to shows, and the only bank holiday when there isn't a show is probably Christmas Day.'

The work of show jumping grooms is tough. If you travel with the horses, there are a lot of early starts and long roads ahead. The aim in show jumping is to get horses upgraded; to do this they must win a lot of money by entering a lot of shows, before they can reach Grade A and go on the international circuit. To achieve this level means spending a lot of time on the county show scene. What you see of show jumpers on the television is only the tip of the iceberg. Last-minute entries into shows at the other end of the country to get a win are not uncommon, and you may find yourself travelling straight from one show to another, grooming and cleaning tack as you go. It's a hectic life but a rewarding one. Emma Storey started riding at the age of three; she has had several ponies of her own and has a lot of Pony Club and competition experience. Emma works for David Broome:

> 'Deep down I've always wanted to work with horses, but when I was younger, people said it's not really a career, there's no money in it, it's hard work and long hours, and there's really nowhere you can go promotion-wise. My parents never really wanted me to work with horses, but that didn't stop me!
>
> 'I've been with David for four years now. The accommodation here is fantastic, I've got a five-bedroom flat with two bathrooms – really nice! He also pays for the bills such as electricity. David is very easy to work for, never any hassle, and my main job is travelling anyway, so I'm not here very often.
>
> 'I get £125 a week in my hand, most grooms get £100–£120. Everyone gets their accommodation paid for. We have to buy our own food, but that doesn't matter much because I'm away so often and David pays for our food when we're travelling. When we're on the road, I live in the lorry, so I don't have to spend much.'

As well as being travelling groom, Emma is also head groom in David's yard and when she isn't on the road, she oversees the running of the yard in David's absence.

> 'Work starts at seven o'clock, when we feed and muck out, finishing at eight. Breakfast is until 8.45, then we're back out riding at nine o'clock. We ride all morning and try to get each horse ridden before lunch. After lunch, the horses get groomed and routine stable chores get done. That's the routine for the yard grooms. I don't have an average day because I'm on the road so much.
>
> 'My main job is looking after David's Grade A horses; when he rides I do them for him. I'm always packing and unpacking! I'm lucky, a large part of my job is travelling around the world.
>
> 'I keep saying to myself, "What am I going to do after?" I have done other things before, so I have other skills to turn to. If I had to give up horses, say because of injury, I'd panic! Then I'd probably go home. Fortunately, my parents have a very good business, so I can always help them until I find something else. At the moment I've no other ambitions; I'm quite happy here.'

TRAVELLING OPPORTUNITIES

In a top yard, travelling is one of the perks. You may have to work while on the road, but the opportunity to see a bit of the world is very rewarding. How far you travel depends on who you work for, and if your employer is successful enough, you may have the opportunity of a lifetime – to go to the Olympics. In 1992, Annie Collings went to the Barcelona Olympics with her charge, Mary Thomson's King William, and the social side of such an event provided some happy memories:

> 'To be part of the British team as a groom is an excellent opportunity. You haven't just got your own horse to look after, you have to think about the other team horses as well. Obviously, you're in control of your own horse – I did everything for William – but there were times when I had to help someone else with their horse.
>
> 'During the various events, the grooms all get together and we have a good time. We had some fantastic parties at the Europeans in Ireland – some got well out of hand! At the Olympics there was nothing planned, so it was what you made of it.'

As a travelling groom, you get to know all the other grooms on the circuit and there is a great deal of camaraderie between grooms and riders.

The life of a travelling groom may sound wonderful, but there is a serious side to the job. You will be responsible for seeing that everything runs smoothly and you will have to relieve some of the pressures on your employer so that they can concentrate on the task of riding successfully.

Preparing horses for travelling means a lot of packing; it's an expensive mistake to forget to pack the right bridle or martingale. You must be sufficiently well organised not to need reminding twice. You won't have much time for riding, but this is compensated for by the privileges of travelling. The responsibilities of a travelling groom are the most important in any competition yard and you will not be offered the position unless you can prove that you are punctual, unflappable and completely reliable, but life on the road isn't all work, as Emma Storey explains:

> 'On the travelling side of the job, I do get the chance to do a lot of sight seeing and socialising. It depends how far we are going. If we travel a long distance we like to get there about two or three days before the show. The horses are rested for a couple of days so we have the chance to go and see places. When I went to Rome, we got there three days before the show. David told us to rest the horses the first day and look round the city. We did the usual tourist thing and went sight-seeing to famous places like the Coliseum, the Spanish Steps and McDonalds!
>
> 'Some of the shows are in the middle of nowhere but most of them are in good places where you can go out. We went to a show in the middle of Paris right under the Eiffel Tower. We had a great time looking round the city. You get a chance to go out; the work's not twenty-four hours a day. I think if it was, you'd crack up. Unlike some travel grooms, I'm lucky to have a box driver, a girl that comes and drives the lorry leaving me to look after the horses.'

Whatever the type of yard you work in, you need one important quality – you must really love horses because your job is to keep them happy. If you love them, you will find groom's work a very worthwhile and enjoyable vocation.

Chapter 3

Further Opportunities

THE COMPETITION RIDER

Competing for a living is the pearl in the equestrian shell. It sounds wonderful, but as professional rider, David Broome explains, it is extremely difficult:

'For many it will remain just a dream. To compete for a living you need support from a lot of angles: family, staff, bank managers etc. – and more than just financial support!'

Before you start up as a competition rider, ask yourself, 'Do I have the backing of my family?' If you have their faith, consider whether you have the financial resources. One option is financial backing from family, a wealthy relative, or your parents or spouse, but few competition riders are in this position and those who are may have the financial resources, but lack the talent. You may have all the money you need to compete, but if you don't have talent, you are unlikely to succeed.

More realistically, if you are prepared to work hard, you can combine competing with paid employment to provide your equestrian expenses as well as money to live on. It has been done, quite successfully, by event rider, Mary Thomson, who has achieved international success and recognition in the eventing world, not because of privilege but because she has talent, bravery and dedication. Mary explains:

> 'I learned to ride on the vicar's pony when I was six. After that, I used to ride whatever ponies I could find in the area that people weren't using. I've always been crazy about horses although my parents aren't horsey at all. Mum has got involved but she still doesn't like touching them much!

'Eventually, I persuaded my parents to get me a pony when I was thirteen. I kept it at the vicarage stable and a farmer let me use his field, because we don't have any land of our own. I competed quite a lot with my own pony. It took a few years to get used to each other because we were both young and inexperienced. However, we got going and turned out to be very successful.

'I left school when I was sixteen, straight after getting seven out of the eight O levels I took. My teachers were furious, they wanted me to stay on and do A levels. I sort of enjoyed school, but I knew all I wanted to do was "horses", so I saw no point in staying on. I sold my pony and went to work for ex-event rider, Sheila Wilcox.

'The job involved breaking in horses and producing the young ones. It was a high-class dealing yard, so I was riding all sorts of horses, all day, every day, for two-and-a-half years and that was really where I learnt my basics. From there I came back home to my parents in Devon and said, "Right, I'm going to event" Mum and Dad haven't got very much money and we have no facilities here but I was keen. I was lucky to find a derelict farmyard and the farmer agreed to let me rent a couple of stables. I bought a horse with the money from the sale of my pony and started from there.

'I set up a small business teaching and I also bought and sold a couple of horses. Then I did all sorts of odd jobs to keep going. Anything and everything, from butcher's delivery rounds twice a week, cleaning campsite loos to digging people's gardens, and I was able to earn quite a lot in those days! The hard part was finding the time to ride. As far as the eventing went, I was fairly successful but I was at the stage where if I got offered a reasonable amount of money for a horse, I'd have to sell it because I couldn't afford to keep it going, although I really wanted to get to the top level.'

Sponsorship

The ideal option is sponsorship but it is also the most difficult. You must first prove that you are suffiently talented and dedicated. Sponsors expect more for their money than just their name on your horsebox.

The competition for sponsorship is hot, so be business-like about presenting yourself to prospective companies. Your local reference library will have a selection of directories listing companies; for example *The Kompass Directory*, which includes the names and addresses of companies, their annual turnover, and the names of the directors.

Ascertain which companies are in a financial position to back you; often equestrian-related companies and those close to home are your best choice. *The Sponsorship Directory* contains the names and addresses of sponsors and grants available throughout the UK.

Submit a letter of introduction and a CV documenting your career and competition successes to date. Present a realistic business plan of what it will cost to sponsor you, say for one year, with one or two horses. Include any press cuttings and professional photos of you in action. Tell prospective sponsors what they can expect for their money by way of publicity and advertising. (The British Equestrian Federation at Stoneleigh should be notified of private sponsorship deals, as they are required to officiate by the Fédération Equestre Internationale.) You can also agree to attend press conferences, and be a celebrity guest and after-dinner speaker at company functions.

Personal contacts already in the sport who are involved with com-panies may help you get in touch with people who are looking for riders to sponsor. Luck plays a large part in this instance, as Mary Thomson discovered in 1985:

> 'I was desperate to find a sponsor, but it's extremely difficult. I eventually fell on my feet, however, when a company called the Carphone Group found out about me. It was all through some people I bought a horse from that were connected to this company. They had heard that the company were wanting to get involved in eventing and said that they knew of somebody (me) who was really keen to get to the top, but couldn't afford to.
>
> 'It went from there and I managed to clinch a sponsorship deal. I had a horse called Diver's Rock, whom I'd been producing since 1982, he was the first horse that I'd had a ride at Badminton on. He was showing terrific potential and then in 1984 I won the award for having the highest points-winning horse through the year. So he'd had a fair bit of success and that spurred the company on to sponsor me.
>
> 'I went to Badminton for the first time running under the Carphone Group name in 1985. The Chairman and his wife came to the event and thought it was just the best thing ever! Coming to the cocktail party at Badminton House, meeting the Duke and Duchess of Beaufort, rubbing shoulders with royalty – it was right up their street! Plus they loved the horses and loved the sport. So that's really where it all started and over the next few years I built up a team of

eight horses, bought for me by the Carphone Group. They went on and sponsored me for four years. I really got going then and had the finances to get more dressage training, and jumping lessons and learn how to do things properly!

'The Carphone Group was bought out by a major worldwide company in 1989 and, unfortunately, the chairman and his wife split up. That chairman's former wife, Gill Robinson, now sponsors me on a personal ownership basis. She owns the horses I have in the yard and pays for their expenses while I carry on riding and producing them.'

Finance – income and outgoings

There's not really a lot of prize money involved in eventing unless you're at the very top level, although things have improved in recent years, as Mary explains:

'Badminton is the top event in the world. During the eighties, first prize was only about £8000, which is nothing when you consider the amount of time and money it takes to produce a horse to that level and enter it. In 1992 Badminton got a new sponsor and the first prize leapt up from £8000 to £20,000 – I won that year, which was a terrific boost! Badminton and Burghley are the two major events with high prize money. At the one-day events, you might get a maximum of £300 first prize but it costs that in expenses to enter and travel to the event.'

Once you find a sponsor, it's a good idea to employ a groom to help with the yard work and exercising so you can concentrate on riding. Mary employs two girls full-time during the season.

'Annie Collings is my experienced girl – she's been with me for nine years now, and over the last few years I've also taken on one working pupil, a younger person who's still learning, on a lower wage . They're both here from January through to October, till the season ends. The grooms take it in turns to come with me to competitions while the other stays at home to do the horses, so you really need two.'

Good grooms are hard to find and even harder to keep. Many professional riders know that if your team is to be a success, you must be a good employer as well as a good rider.

> 'We're like a happy family, very much a team and working together. It's not really a case of "the boss" and "the employees", although I suppose it can a bit; we're ever such good friends. We go on holiday together and all sorts, I'm very lucky.
>
> 'The grooms work a six day week. At home, we have a pretty civilised start time of eight a.m. The horses are fed and mucked out. Then the riding starts. I do all the schooling and jumping. The girls will help me do all the extra fitness work, like road work. If they're good enough riders, they do some of the fast work. We try and get as many horses as possible worked in the morning.
>
> 'After the horses are worked they get turned out in the field for an hour, whatever the weather. Lunch is from one till two o'clock. After lunch, the grooms work through the afternoon, which is when all the extra horses that haven't been worked are ridden. Then it's grooming, tack cleaning and any odd jobs that need doing, such as tidying the horses, pulling and trimming manes and general jobs, such as cleaning mangers, windows etc.
>
> 'The girls finish off by watering and skipping-out at five o'clock. I like to do the evening haying and feeding because I enjoy being on my own with the horses at this time.'

There's a lot more to competing than yard work and riding: you have to keep up with the business side of things as well which includes a lot of paper work so it helps to be organised.

FURTHER OPPORTUNITIES

Success as a competition rider means in effect you become a business. The career expectancy of sports personalities, both human and equine, can be cut short by injury. You have to make the most of business opportunities to increase your bank balance and ensure long-term security.

'I don't have to buy and sell any more to keep going because luckily my sponsor, Gill, is very kind,' explains Mary. 'We have an agreement that she keeps the trophies and I keep the prize money, which is now my main income. I do a couple of teaching clinics throughout the year as well as lecture demonstrations and I earn quite a bit.'

There could also be the chance to write articles for magazines which would enhance your profile and earn some extra income. Famous names on covers help sell books, so it's worth thinking about writing a book. Angles can vary: an autobiography, a practical guide based on your knowledge and training, a biography of a horse with whom you have achieved international recognition, or you could come up with a new concept. You may not think you have the necessary skills to write a book yourself, but often successful riders are approached by writers so that the two can combine their resources.

Marketing people are always interested in successful sports personalities to put their names to their products. In the horse industry, it is usually the associated trades, such as food, clothing and insurance which pay competitors to promote their products.

International Competitions

The icing on the cake for any successful sports competitor has to be representing your country in the Olympics. Mary was chosen for the British three-day-event team for the Barcelona Olympics in 1992.

'The Olympics were a great challenge and very exiting. We had a fantastic time out there, even though our event didn't go as well as we hoped by any means. It was all quite disappointing, but the rest of the Olympics was just brilliant.'

Riders are picked for the Olympics as much for the ability and soundness of their horses as for their own talents, and getting a horse to the Olympics takes a lot of training and good stable management.

> 'After winning Badminton Horse Trials with King William, it was only eleven weeks until the Olympics, which was frighteningly close. After Badminton, the horses normally have six weeks' complete holiday after such a stressful event but William only had two weeks' holiday and then had to start working again. Luckily, he's a very strong horse with terrific natural energy and power and Badminton didn't take much out of him.
>
> 'Following his two-week rest, I built up his work again. There was a final trial at the beginning of July, which all the horses short-listed for the Olympics had to run at. It was purely a fitness run; the selectors knew who they wanted on the team and we just had to go around carefully and produce a good, clear round and not do anything heroic in case the horses knocked themselves. From the final trial, the team plus two reserves went into training for ten days

at Badminton House.

'After training, horses and riders were flown out to the Olympics. The atmosphere was amazing. The grooms, unfortunately, were stuck out with the horses but we made sure they had a couple of chances to come down and see the Olympic village and stadium and watch some of the other events. It really is an experience to remember, for everyone!'

If you're going to compete for a living, you must be honest with yourself. All our top riders vary in their financial status and background, but the one thing they all have in common is talent. Are you really talented enough to compete successfully, or is it just a dream? If you are talented enough, then a combination of hard work, dedication and a measure of luck should see you through.

WORKING ABROAD

The British groom, like the British nanny or butler, is perceived as a great asset in foreign countries. Most people think there is no other country in the world that can match the standards of the British horse societies' and associations' training of grooms, instructors, racing and stud staff.

Although some other countries like Germany and Norway have their own system of training staff, Britain can still claim to set the standard when it comes to turning out well-trained staff, and those who are truly dedicated and love the horses.

The European Union

Under the new European Union (EU) regulations, much of the 'red tape' which used to accompany working in Europe has been removed. You must apply for a residence permit, which you will automatically receive, but you and your family no longer need work permits. You also have the right to establish yourself as a self-employed person in an EU member state. In that event, your rights are basically the same as those of an employed person and you will not need a work permit. You may, however, have to comply with the conditions placed on that country's nationals for the type of business concerned.

As a national of a EU country, you are entitled to take a job or to set up a business anywhere in the EU. Your spouse, your children under twenty-one, and other dependent relatives enjoy a similar right. This applies even if they are not themselves EU nationals, provided that you are working.

Of course, being able to work or run your own business in another EU country ('a host country') is still difficult if your qualifications are not recognised, or if you have to re-qualify once you are there.

To deal with this problem, the EU has adopted a series of measures (directives) aimed at ensuring qualifications and training obtained in one member state will be recognised in every member state, subject to certain conditions. EU rules are designed to help you use any formal qualifications or practical experience gained in your 'home' in order to meet the host country's requirements to enter a profession. This is being achieved by three initiatives:

- In some cases, the content of training courses has been harmonised; for example, a vet in Scotland will receive the same basic training as a vet in France. This allows for the mutual recognition of qualifications between member states.
- In other cases, a EU Certificate of Experience is available to show that you have had experience of a trade or profession of between three to five years. This allows, for example, grooms, stud staff or people in the racing industry to rely on their experience in their home country when they move to other EU countries to work.
- Finally, with regard to qualifications such as the BHS exams, which are awarded by an internationally recognised governing body, there is the First General System of Mutual Recognition of Qualifications which came into force in January 1991. It obliges each EU country to recognise qualifications obtained in other member states, even where the content of the studies is quite different – subject to certain conditions. At the moment, this system applies only to qualifications granted after at least three years post-secondary education. This includes agriculture, veterinary work, leatherwork, retail and leisure.

The BHS, as Britain's senior authoritative body concerning equestrian teaching, has done some good work on the comparability of qualifications with many other equivalent organisations in Europe; an update on this on-going work can be obtained from the BHS Training and Education Office at Stoneleigh.

Even though your qualifications will be recognised in every EU member state, it is vital to have some knowledge of the local language.

You must be able to contact professional bodies abroad, to get through job interviews and to complete any aptitude test which you may be required to pass. However, the level of knowledge that can be required will vary, according to the type of work you are doing.

To get a job in another EU member state you may use all the usual channels e.g., *Horse and Hound*, employment agencies, as well as personal contacts already living abroad. There is also an EU service which may be able to help you. It is called SEDAN and it keeps up-to-date information on vacancies throughout the Union. You can use it by calling in at any Job Centre in the UK.

The best way to find work is often to travel out to the country you are interested in, and you are entitled to remain in other EU member states for a 'reasonable time' for that purpose. Although this period varies from country to country, generally speaking, it is about three months. You may remain longer if you can prove you are still looking for a job and you have a genuine chance of getting one. This is one of your best chances of finding employment because you are 'on the spot' for the normal interviewing procedures, as you would be at home, and so you are in a better position to negotiate terms and conditions. In certain circumstances, you may transfer your UK National Insurance benefits to another country, but you cannot transfer means-tested benefits, such as income support or family credit.

Going abroad

Working abroad provides opportunities for travel, self-expansion and the chance to learn from the different skills and expertise found in other countries. For example, we often think of Germany as setting the standard in dressage. Some countries, such as Switzerland, offer a higher level of wages, although the cost of living in such countries can be higher. If it's sunny climates you want, you could try one of the Mediterranean countries. However, some countries do not allow foreigners to just 'swan in' and start working. It is difficult to get work permits in non-EU states, so this must be investigated before leaving home.

There may also be work in Australia and New Zealand, and across the Atlantic. America thinks very highly of British equestrian qualifications. Josephine Tyack, BHSPI, has previously worked in America, and once she has passed her BHSII, she intends to return:

> 'When I first went to California, I started off in a training yard teaching people and schooling horses, mainly American

Thoroughbreds, off the track, to sell them on as competition horses. I came back with the intention of getting my BHS Instructors' qualifications so that I can go back again and get an even better job equipped with my BHSII. America doesn't have a national certificate for riding instructors and they appreciate the BHS qualifications a lot more than the British do.

'Everybody in the States has a trainer; on the West Coast in particular. You don't ride your horse without a trainer if you are competing. Trainers out there make so much money. One girl I knew, about twenty one, who didn't particularly blow me away with her teaching skills, had a group of six girls to train. The money she charged them was amazing! Then she'd take them to shows and charge them another fee for horse show training. That's what inspired me to come back to Britain and get qualified.

'Because America has no system of instructors' exams, people don't know if their trainers are good at their profession or bogus "cowboys". With a BHS qualification, you can show you've reached a competitive standard of stable management, riding and instruction. Then it's a case of building on your reputation by word of mouth.'

Once you've passed your exams in Britain and/or gained experience with good references to prove such, then you may wish to expand your knowledge and experience by working abroad. Before you take a job abroad, it's important to find out about the person you will be working for and also if the job they are offering is genuine. There have been cases of people going to work abroad to find the job advertised is not the same as the job they are expected to do, or worse, there is no job at all. You must find at least two referees to provide character references of your prospective employer. They could be fellow colleagues in the sport, or professional associates, such as their accountant or doctor.

Financing your journey is another important matter which you must clarify with your employer – before you embark! When you go overseas, you will need either some guarantee, in writing, that the employer will pay your return fare if you're not happy, or you will have to take sufficient funds with you to get back.

Once you've confirmed your position and made sure you have the means to get home if things don't work out, remember to take out medical insurance before you leave the UK. In other countries, medical and dental fees are very costly. Remember, you'll be working in a high-risk occupation, so you can't afford to take chances. There's nothing worse than being stranded in another country with a broken leg, no relatives close by and an employer who takes the view that because you're now unfit for the job, you're no longer in his employ – it has happened!

Josephine warns:

> 'Although the wages are much better abroad, you have no National Health Service and that completely throws you back, I didn't take out an insurance policy before I went to the States – a classic mistake. I should have bought holiday insurance. One day, I cut my little finger on a cat food tin; it was really deep and I had to have it stitched together which cost me $1000. Imagine what it would have cost me if I'd broken my leg! You also have to pay a lot more for dental treatment, so get a check-up with your NHS dentist before you go.'

Get a work permit. In one case, two girls flew to America to go to a job but they had no work permit and were turned round at the airport and sent home; it was an expensive mistake! Horror stories aside, working abroad can be financially rewarding, a lot of fun and provide an excellent chance to improve your skills and knowledge while seeing something of the world. There are good employers abroad as well as bad, just as there are in this country – it's up to you to take measures to avoid the bad!

One good way of having a taste of the USA is to work in a BUNA Camp, which is a children's horse riding holiday camp; such jobs are advertised every year in the British press. They include some weeks for sight-seeing at the end of the summer.

One of the attractions of working abroad are the better wages and conditions on offer, explains Josephine Tyack:

> 'Compared with America, the pay and conditions for instructors over here are awful, When I started work over there, I had to start at the lowest level, but even then I was better paid than the average in Britain. Some overseas salaries include insurance cover in the contract. Most good companies will automatically cover you with health insurance. But a lot of trainers' jobs out there are on a self-employed basis. So although you will be earning all those dollars in training fees, if you break your wrist or need a couple of fillings, that cash would soon get swallowed up. Individual insurance costs quite a lot; doing it through your employer may get you reduced rates.
>
> 'Finally you will need public liability insurance: the girl trainer I

mentioned had to buy insurance to cover a million dollars worth of accident claim, just for teaching! It is well worth it, though, once you've reached a certain level and can earn hundreds of dollars in your training sessions!'

Associated trades

If you are not interested in riding or looking after horses, or if you want to give up groom's work, instead of wasting all the skills and knowledge you have acquired why not re-direct yourself into one of the many horse-associated activities. If you are disabled, it may be that you want to work in the horse industry but are physically unable to work directly with horses, in which case a job that relates to horses will provide you with great interest and satisfaction.

A lot of people come to horses later in life and if you have been made redundant and have always been interested in horses, you could adapt your previous qualifications and experience to working in the horse industry.

If you have not yet left school, then make the most of your education while it is free and take every opportunity to learn things that will help you in your long-term career plans, such as business, creative, secretarial or computer studies. If you are currently working with horses and thinking about a change of direction, why not take up evening classes? There are home study courses available for almost any type of occupation, as well as GSCE courses and Open University courses which may be useful if you are in a rural area. To study at home, you need a lot of commitment and self-discipline to complete the course – it's not easy to study if you have been working a long day in the yard.

It may be wiser to give up your job and take on a full-time course at college as a mature student or go on a Government-funded adult training scheme. Giving up working with horses often means giving up the roof over your head as well, so you need to find somewhere to stay while you are studying. Renting a flat isn't cheap and you will also have costly bills to pay. Groom's work may not be brilliantly paid, but at least it takes the pressure off where the cost of living is concerned.

Financial Help

Some of the following courses mentioned are grant-aided or pay a small apprenticeship wage. Those who do not qualify can apply for a Career Development Loan, available through a partnership arrangement between the Department of Employment and some high street banks. For further details ask at your local Employment Service office.

Choices

Your own talents, preferences and skills already acquired will help you choose which of the following occupations to pursue.

Farriery

'No foot – no horse' is a very wise saying. Farriery is one of the few remaining hand crafts which still provides a good income as well as a lot of job satisfaction. These days a good farrier is worth the weight of his anvil in gold.

Despite the abundance of work, a career in farriery should not be undertaken lightly. It involves a lot of back bending and having the patience and skill to deal with fractious animals (most farriers retire between forty and sixty years old due to stress on their back). Horses' feet vary considerably in size, shape and defects for a variety of reasons like poor conformation and long-term injury. A good farrier should possess a sound knowledge of both theory and practice of the craft. For information on training as a farrier, see page 149.

Journalism and Publishing

For many, the training for a career in journalism starts in childhood with making up stories and writing about day-to-day events. If you enjoy writing and are good at English, then you may want to combine your interest in writing with your knowledge of horses. Journalism is an extremely competitive field as many people are attracted to what seems like a glamorous life. The image of journalists spending most of their day at long, boozy lunches is very far from the truth and if you wish to succeed you must be committed, determined and hard-working. Talent is important but training is also necessary. The writers' craft is not as easy as it looks. Colleges of Further Education, writer's schools and home study courses offer the opportunity to learn to write professionally.

There are many personal qualities required for a career in journalism. An enquiring mind and a genuine interest in your subject, coupled with gutsy doggedness and determination to follow up a story are vital. Recognising a good story, research (which is eighty per cent of the job) and writing clear, concise, accurate copy will make your articles marketable. Interviewing skills and the ability to win the confidence of all types of people, and healthy challenging of figures of authority are essential for good journalism. The ability to look at a story from all points of view will ensure that the copy you write will not be one-sided.

There are few opportunities for equestrian journalists on a salaried basis with the numerous equestrian magazines; it is more usual to work as a freelance, which gives greater scope to sell your work but requires self-confidence and an ability to motivate yourself. When writing articles you must be able to write for a specific market – it's no use writing to please yourself. Study the equestrian magazines – they vary enormously in their readership. You can get a clear picture of that magazine's readers by studying the advertisements and readers' letters that appear in current issues. Keep a mental picture of a reader in your mind and write the article for that reader. Editors are always open to new ideas, so long as they appeal to their readers. Make it a priority to learn to touch-type, as this makes producing work a lot faster.

Magazines are prepared months in advance. Editors decide when features on subjects such as breeding, hunting or showing will appear, and a good journalist will co-operate with editors to come up with suitable stories – on time! A good equestrian journalist can also offer to help authorities and personalities within the industry to write books.

Editorial vacancies in magazines are usually filled by people who have had a considerable amount of experience in media work. Journalism and publishing experience, a liking for horses and a knowledge of desk top publishing (DTP) are essential. You must be able to anticipate needs and recognise trends if your magazine is going to remain popular and increase sales. Building up good relationships with your staff to inspire a good team spirit are vital. Sales staff can only sell advertising space with the help of good editorials which attract the readers that advertisers are trying to reach.

Production, which includes advertising design and graphic layout of the magazine, is another opening, particularly for those with DTP and graphic design skills. There are also a few openings in publishing companies who specialise in, or have a department for, equestrian books, both technical and fiction. All the careers centred around journalism, photography and publishing need proper training, creative talent and preferably some experience with local newspapers or the trade press.

There are different ways of getting into journalism and publishing. However, regardless of your educational qualifications, you will probably have to start at the bottom and work your way up. There is no right way to start. Some of the top journalists and editors in publishing, for example, have degrees, some have A levels, some have a more vocational qualification like a NCTJ Diploma or secretarial certificate.

You could also try starting in journalism and publishing through the secretarial route. Many brilliant writers and editors started off their careers as secretaries. If you are just starting out and looking for a way of breaking into journalism, you may stand your best chance of getting in if you apply for a secretarial job. No-one will take you on as a writer or editor until you have some experience behind you. Finally, every magazine needs people to sell advertising space; much of this work is done on the telephone. It is a daunting task but it could be a beginning.

Photography

You can train as a photographer at art college or learn the ropes from an established photographer, preferably on a youth training scheme. With proper training and talent, you can earn a good living as a photographer in the horse industry, particularly if you do the rounds of the horse shows taking photos of competitors and sending them samples to order from. As in journalism, however, the competition is intense and you will need to supplement your income by producing work for non-equestrian publications until you are well established in the equestrian field.

Police and Army

If service life appeals, there are opportunities for working with horses in the Army and police force, both as civilians and soldiers/officers.

In the police force, officers have to complete two years on the beat before being able to apply to become a Mounted Branch officer; the force also employs civilian staff in their stables and training establishments. Not every constabulary has a mounted branch, the Metropolitan Division being the largest employer in this field.

The Army can offer a wide range of training opportunities, including instruction in a number of horse-related trades. There are several regiments to which you can apply, the main ones being the Royal Army Veterinary Corps and the Royal Horse Artillery. Your local Army Careers Information Office will be able to help you.

Marketing

Marketing has been defined as 'producing a product that does not come back, for customers who do' and neglecting this area of the business has been the downfall of many equestrian ventures. Some people have a flair for marketing and are constantly coming up with ideas that sell and keep selling as well as providing sound promotional concepts, following them through every stage of their development and keeping up good public relations with the companies that sell these products. Marketing is a co-ordinated job – it's like being a mini managing director for a brand or product. With any new idea it is the marketing person who is solely responsible for liaising with packaging, finance, sales and production and co-ordinating it all. A marketing person is a Jack of many trades, master of turning ideas into profit.

The skills for marketing work include a thorough knowledge of finance because a lot of the work is concerned with profit, so you need to know about break-even point, profit and loss etc. You need an element of creative flair and a sound knowledge of advertising. You also need to appreciate production problems – can you make it bigger, longer, shorter, wider or sooner? The best way is to get some sort of grounding by working in different areas.

Training

The traditional route into marketing is up through the sales force, and you can get into the marketing department with very little formal training as such, because you don't necessarily need a lot of qualifications to be good at selling. Also, this way you see exactly what happens at the front end of the business. The new tradition, however, is to attend college or university to get a degree or diploma, then hopefully try and get into a marketing department. You can do an Higher National Diploma or degree in Business Studies, which will include modules in marketing but you cannot get a marketing degree on its own. You may prefer to take an HND or BA degree in Horses and Business Management.

The problem with marketing, like everything else, is that on the job front you can't get into marketing till you've got the experience, and they won't give you the experience until you've got in – it may seem an impenetrable circle. Therefore, training-wise, the best option is a sandwich course whereby your degree runs over four years instead of three. After two years, you do one year of practical experience on placement with a company, then complete your final year at college and, not only will you have the degree, but some experience as well. Some of the courses will help place you during your degree and then you are on a better footing when you apply for jobs.

Personal qualities

You need to be outgoing – enjoy talking to people. You've also got to be able to roll with the punches. A lot of people won't want to talk to you at all. In marketing, you tend to deal with people who are more senior than you, so you need tenacity. Of course, you will get the kudos that goes with a good deal. Marketing is the cream of business, it is a highly paid and very enjoyable career.

Creativity is important, but not so important that you are blinded by it. In marketing, you've got to see a project from other people's points of view; it's a tough business.

Opportunities

Once you've got a degree and a bit of work experience, you have to go out and find a job. Sitting back and waiting is the wrong thing to do. Sure, jobs will be advertised and you can go for them. What you've got to do is actually go out and try and sell your skills. If you can't market yourself you'll not be able to market horses and equestrian products. You must sell why you are needed. Look around at the industry, look at the companies within it. See what they're doing, see what they're not doing, come up with ideas, make suggestions. You've got to be cost-effective. Nobody is going to employ you if you cost them £10,000 and they only make £5,000 out of your ideas.

Write to companies and offer your services. Apply for jobs that aren't advertised on the basis that the company might be thinking of advertising for someone soon; your application may start them thinking. Going self-employed straight away is a big danger. It's okay once you've had some experience, but if you go self-employed in marketing, straight from college, for example, you've had no practical experience. Companies will usually want somebody who has a proven record.

However, once you've had some experience, setting up a marketing agency tailored specifically for the horse industry is an idea – particularly at the lower end of the scale. In the equestrian side of the horse industry, quite a lot of businesses might not want a full-time marketing person, it might not be cost effective. What they may want is somebody perhaps two or three days a month. If you're prepared to adjust and move around a bit – this could be beneficial, from both sides.

Convincing people that they need a marketing consultant is very difficult; it means persuading people to spend money when they don't want to spend it, and a lot of people don't think they need marketing because they come up with ideas anyway. With regard to the horse industry, one argument could be, 'the more competition you get, the more you need to run the place like a business, therefore the more you need marketing skills. It's the people who don't use the marketing skills available to find out what customers actually want who are going to go under, particularly in a recession.'

So many equestrian businesses are run for pleasure rather than profit, people don't realise they can have both. The first element of any marketing skill is talking to the customers, but a lot of people forget this. Instead they tell the customer, 'This is what I've got.' which is not the way marketing works. You've got to say to the customer, 'What do you want?', then try to tailor the business towards the reply.

You'll need to persuade people that they need a marketing consultant. Most equestrian business are too busy just trying to break even to think about investing in marketing. Adapt your skills in marketing to the horse industry; start by doing your research. Who are the customers? What do they want? Where are they? To quote Rudyard Kipling's philosophy, 'I have six honest serving men – they've taught me all I know. Their names are What and Where and When, and Why and How and Who.'

Although marketing should be on-going, that doesn't necessarily mean coming up with new ideas. The ideas don't have to be revolutionary; they can be something really simple. For example, at a riding school why not offer a crèche facility one afternoon a week. Some mothers may want to ride, but don't have anyone to look after the kids – all of a sudden you've got fifty people who might now be free to come horse riding.

Marketing is pure common sense – the trouble is not enough equestrian businesses use it even though an awful lot need it. Successful marketing is simply about talking to customers and finding out what they want.

Retail

Direct selling from manufacturer to retail outlets provides many people with their first taste of selling. Fewer qualifications are required in selling than in practically any other area. However, you need to be a certain sort of animal to sell, the sort of person who can take fifty-seven 'no's' and still go and see the fifty-eighth person. To some extent selling is a knack, but it can be learnt. You need unsquashable confidence, enthusiasm and thorough knowledge of your product – then you can do it.

Real selling is not about persuading people to do anything other than what they wanted to do already. You just lead them along the path gently, 'You wanted this, you wanted that – this product provides it.' But if you've got the wrong basic product, then life will be twice as tough. You need to be able to take all the hard knocks; some managers will deliberately leave you standing around for hours – just to show you they're the boss.

The retail trade within the horse industry offers you a chance to set up in business, perhaps selling saddlery, clothing and accessories, either by running a shop or setting up a trade stand at shows and venues around the country. Experience in this field could come from working for a company which may be outside the equestrian industry. Many companies and large department stores now offer on-going training for sales staff where you can learn about buying stock, selling techniques, business and personnel management – all of which can be successfully adapted to working in the horse industry.

Saddlery

Saddlery, like farriery is a highly rewarding ancient and respected craft which can trace the existence of a guild of saddlers back to the late twelfth century. However, the traditional method of craft training – by apprenticeship to a Master saddler – is in decline. The Government has now made the National Council for Vocational Qualifications responsible for implementing a system of vocational qualifications through existing educational and training organisations.

The Worshipful Company of Saddlers, together with the Society of Master Saddlers and the City & Guilds of London Institute have developed the necessary assessment procedures and qualification levels for use by the saddlery trade throughout the UK. This scheme covers workers in the saddlery craft who are involved in the manufacture of saddlery, bridlework and harness, at levels from trainee to Master. The governing bodies of saddlery, mentioned above, are responsible for operating this scheme on behalf of the JNHETC, which itself is responsible for setting the standards of all training programmes within the horse industry. For more details of saddlery courses available, see page 151.

Secretarial

The opportunities for secretarial work within the horse industry are plentiful and varied. You can, if you wish, find a post that combines the usual nine to five secretarial duties with, perhaps, a couple of hours' riding. For example, a racehorse trainer's secretary could ride out first and second lot before taking up his or her office duties. It gives you the best of both worlds, but you must have the necessary qualifications and experience. Copy- or audio-typing, filing, book-keeping and general office practice are all necessary skills. Computers are now a vital asset in many offices, so word processing and database experience will improve your chances of employment considerably.

All this training can be done while you are still at school or college, but if you have already left, there are plenty of training agencies in towns and cities throughout the country that offer adult and youth training at RSA or Pitman and NVQ levels. Most people will gain their training by progressing from school to college. Some will take a horse course and then top it up with extra secretarial training; you can do a short course or evening classes at your local college or take a home study course.

Working in the office of a professional yard doesn't offer much in the way of promotion, but the work is usually better paid than groom's work with fewer hours and less physical 'graft'. Often, you may have accommodation included, with the opportunity of riding available.

There are also opportunities within the various governing bodies and associations of the horse industry. These posts are often advertised in *Horse and Hound* where 'an interest in and knowledge of horses would be an advantage' is mentioned in the advert.

Secretarial skills are a good back-up if you are in groom's work and find yourself having to give up, say because of injury. Jobs in this field are abundant and a good way of gaining experience in secretarial work is to sign up with a temping agency. The wages are good, and on-going training is always available with some of the larger companies. Secretarial opportunities in the horse industry can also be found by sending a letter of introduction and a CV to the larger equestrian organisations, who may often find staff replacements in-house or through contacts. Making yourself known in this way shows enthusiasm and initiative, qualities which are vital to secretarial work. Finally, as with direct work with horses, training and experience in the industry's associated trades also provides opportunities for the self-employed.

Chapter 4

The Racing Industry

If you want to work with horses but are unsure about what you want to do, don't dismiss a career in racing. It offers far more than the slim chance of becoming a jockey. Racing is the only aspect of direct work with horses that provides a recommended wage, and it now offers youngsters the opportunity to train at one of two racing schools, which not only teach you how to ride racehorses, but also to work to a very high standard of stable management and turnout, providing an excellent basis to your career. Looking after racehorses gives you the chance to work in a professional yard where you will learn to ride extremely well, particularly young and difficult horses – consequently racing also provides an excellent basis for anyone who wants to ride professionally or break-in and train young horses for a living.

The fabric of racing consists of breeding, rearing, buying and selling and the training and racing of Thoroughbred horses. The sport is divided into flat racing and National Hunt racing (which includes hurdle and steeplechasing).

The Framework of Racing Associations

The British Horseracing Board (BHB) is the new governing authority for racing in Great Britain, and replaces some of the duties of the Jockey Club. It is responsible for race planning, racecourse policy, finance and industry consultations.

The Jockey Club retains its wide powers of discipline, and is responsible for issuing trainers and jockeys with licences. The Jockey Club is responsible for keeping the sport on the 'straight and narrow', with the power to fine or suspend jockeys and trainers who step out of line. It also licenses racecourses and clerks of the course, and is responsible for the employment and direction of the Field Force, comprising more than 120 officials on racecourses, the approval and registration of individual owners and companies, and for security on racecourses. It lays down regulations for point-to-point racing, the amateur version of steeplechasing.

Clerks of the scales, handicappers, inspectors of courses, starters, stewards' secretaries, judges, veterinary officers and security staff, are all employed by the Jockey Club. Positions as course officials do not often become available and vacancies are advertised in the racing press. It is considered preferable for applicants to be over thirty years of age and to have some previous experience within the racing industry. Those who are successful undergo a training period of up to twelve months.

The Jockey Club Graduate Development Scheme offers long vacation placements in the summer to a limited number of students, men and women. The placements are intended mainly for students who have completed two years at university, and who have a serious interest in a career in racing or a connected industry. The vacation placements are preceded by a residential course at the British Racing School at Newmarket. The course serves not only to introduce people interested in racing to the workings of the industry, but also to give them an unrivalled opportunity to obtain the information which will enable them to perform well when applying for a permanent job in racing. Contact the Jockey Club for further information.

The Racing and Thoroughbred Breeding Training Board (RTBTB) is a much needed acquisition to the industry. It is in charge of the National Vocational Qualifications within racing. All sixteen- to eighteen-year-olds who come into racing now have to be registered on the Youth Training Scheme and sit NVQs, which can be done either with a trainer or at one of the British Racing Schools.

Candidates have an initial trial period of between four and six weeks in the yard, to see whether they are suitable and like racing enough to go forward to one of the schools. Once the trial period is over, they can attend one of the racing schools where they will have a further eight or nine weeks' intensive training. They will then go back onto the yard, and during the next eighteen to twenty-four months, they will hopefully pass Level I and II of their NVQs.

The Thoroughbred Breeders Association (TBA) co-ordinates the breeding of racehorses. It offers advice to anyone wishing to pursue a career in the bloodstock industry. It will also supply literature on courses available for the Thoroughbred industry throughout the country, and issues potential stud workers with a list of TBA members willing to employ students. The TBA will help students by trying to place them either on studs or in bloodstock agencies.

Weatherbys is the civil service of the racing industry. Records of racing were published as long ago as 1670, and in 1773 Mr James Weatherby first published the Racing Calendar. Ever since then, Messrs Weatherbys have been solicitors, treasurers and secretariat to the Jockey Club, and their responsibilities also include entries, forfeits and declarations for races; the General Stud Book; registration of owners, colours and horses; accountancy and insurance services to owners, trainers and jockeys; publication of an historical database of racing and breeding; and printing race cards. In addition to secretarial and clerical staff, they employ staff for the firm's extensive computer operations.

The Horserace Totalisator Board (The Tote) is the only organisation permitted to operate pool betting on horseracing, and it employs a large number of staff to provide this service, and credit betting, on all racecourses, as well as at many point-to-points.

The Horse Race Betting Levy Board is the financial body of the industry. It is responsible to the Home Office for collecting a levy from betting, and distributing it for the benefit of racing. Most of its staff are employed on levy collection, but there are a few positions devoted to levy distribution to such areas as prize money, racecourse modernisation, security and technical services.

The Stable Lads Association (SLA) was formed in 1975. A completely independent body, it is not connected to, or affiliated to any other organisation. All the leading members of the association are current or ex-stable staff, work riders or trainers. All the SLA National Committee members work within racing and are employed stable staff. The SLA also has Area Committees made up of lads working full-time for trainers.

One of the great advantages of working in racing is that you can join the association, which seeks to ensure that stable staff are protected within the laws of employment, as well as under the rules of racing laid down by the Jockey Club. Unfortunately, the SLA only covers the racing industry, but it does mean that racing stable staff are far better paid and looked after than many grooms in the non-Thoroughbred industry.

The national secretary of the SLA acts on behalf of the members, and is responsible for engaging in talks with employers on all points of confrontation which may occur between employer and employee. The SLA also sees that its members are protected in cases of redundancy, ensuring that stable staff receive their full entitlements. It also deals with many cases of staff who have suffered injury whilst at work, and ensures that stable staff are made aware of the Racing Industry Accident Benefit Scheme. In many instances the SLA will act as a go-between on behalf of staff with their claims.

In taking good care of its members, the SLA also negotiates annually the wages and conditions for the forthcoming year on behalf of all racing's stable staff. It continues to check racecourse accommodation and has, within the last six years, seen wonderful improvements to many hostels around the country. The SLA also campaigned for and gained SOS emergency stations on the Newmarket Heath gallops, as well as seeing a marked improvement in accident procedure in Lambourn.

The SLA has done much during the last six years to improve the life of stable lads. You should not be afraid to protest if all is not right with your working conditions, and the SLA should help you in this, provided you are a member. The SLA will give advice to any stable lad who contacts them, but unless they pay a subscription, the association is unable to act on their behalf. It must be said that many people who fall into this category need help, but are unable to join the SLA because of fear of their employer or because they can't afford the subscription.

Career Prospects

Racing has a high public profile and is one of the most popular televised sports, which is why it attracts youngsters from all walks of life, particularly those who have had little or no direct contact with horses.

Most youngsters who come into racing do so because they want to be jockeys. Only a very small percentage actually make the grade, the rest either stay in racing as stable lads (in racing you're a stable lad whether you're male, female, sixteen or sixty), move on to other aspects of the horse industry, or sadly, give up horses altogether.

Racing isn't just a career, like all aspects of the horse industry, it takes over your life completely. You think, eat and sleep racing. If you have the right attitude and attributes, a career in racing is one of the most rewarding aspects of the horse world.

As well as offering a recommended wage, it also provides allowances for travelling with horses and at race meetings, prizes for best turned out range from £25 to £100. A percentage of the yard's winnings, 'pool money', is also divided between stable staff at the end of the season. The opportunities for promotion and diversification are very good and travel prospects are excellent. You will be able to travel to race meetings around the country and possibly overseas, which is one of the most enjoyable features of the job. The opportunity to work abroad is also very good. Many countries throughout the world have their own racing industry, and it is well known that British stable lads are among the best in the world. Even if you don't wish to stay in racing, the high standards of riding, stable management and turn-out you learn in this job will be of immense benefit throughout your career with horses.

Recruitment

In recent years there has been a scarcity of youngsters coming into racing yards. Many who did come in, stayed for a couple of years, got disillusioned and gave up altogether.

Peter Compton is Education and Training Officer of the National Trainers Federation and the British Racing School. His main responsibility is to recruit youngsters into the sport through liaison with career officers around the country over job opportunities in the industry. Peter is keen to recruit the right calibre of youngsters into the sport:

'Racing wants to attract good quality youngsters. By quality, I don't mean A levels; I mean hard-working youngsters who are dedicated, loyal and genuinely love working with horses.'

To work in racing requires a very special type of person. Stable lads drift in and out of racing like the tide, and the industry is finding it harder to recruit the right sort of youngsters, as Peter explains:

> 'Since I've started this job, we're coming to accept the fact that the youngsters available are not always the type that want, or are equipped to work in racing. Attitudes have changed because society is changing. Also diets have changed so we have a problem with finding youngsters of the right weight. We really are after a very narrow, specialised field of recruits. Not only because of the weight restriction, but also by the very nature of the job, which is demanding both physically and mentally. You've got to be really well-equipped to face the fact that, if you come into this work, it takes over your life. The hours are long, you are working weekends and you have to be thoroughly dedicated to get the job done. You've got to come down in the morning at six-thirty, muck out, sweep up, tack up, ride and feed, even before you sit down and have breakfast. An awful lot of youngsters will look at the work and baulk at it.'

Racing hasn't changed much in its attitude towards stable staff. Employers still expect you to get up early and work hard – there's nothing wrong with that, it's part of the way of life. Anyone coming into this work from a different sort of background will get an almighty shock when they go to work in a yard.

'There are good youngsters about,' believes Peter, 'particularly from the poorer parts of industrial cities or from impoverished backgrounds. These youngsters come into racing with no experience of horses at all and stick out the course, and they've had to work very hard to reach the required standard.'

Years ago, racing was a predominantly male environment; today there is a much larger percentage of girls in racing than ever before.

'The boys that come here all want to be jockeys,' explains Peter. 'That leads to a problem because very few will make the grade. The girls like to work with horses and not all of them want to be jockeys. They are happy just working with the horses so are more likely to stay in racing.'

If you love racing as well as horses, don't let its male-orientated image put you off; girls are just as welcome and just as capable. Racehorses are very highly strung and some, particularly fillies, are sweeter to handle if a girl looks after them. There are many trainers who prefer to have girls instead of boys, for a number of reasons. Usually girls come from a horsey background or they know a bit about stable management. Trainers don't want to have to give instruction from that point of view.

There are opportunities in the industry to expand into all sorts of jobs. Racing is now seen as a better prospect than previously because of the introduction of the NVQs. By taking these exams, you can work your way up in a racing yard. If you're in the right yard or prepared to move around to gain experience and promotion, then you are going to get on. If you have the necessary qualities and meet the criteria it is a very rewarding career.

Training

Racing now comes under the jurisdiction of the Joint National Horse Education and Training Council (JNHETC), which, together with the Racing and Thoroughbred Breeding Training Board (RTBTB) has produced National Vocational Qualifications (see Chapter Eight for details) to meet the specific training needs of the racing industry. In 1993, a new comprehensive training scheme was established for the whole of the racing industry. If you are under nineteen years of age, you will be registered on the industry's Youth Training Programme. The preliminary period of training (up to three months) is spent with a racehorse trainer followed by nine to ten weeks at one of the two racing schools.

Once you have demonstrated your commitment to working with racehorses during your preliminary training, you will then attend one of the two racing schools for a nine- to ten-week course. Here, you should reach NVQ level I standard (the basic qualification), and learn the rudiments of NVQ level II. Once you have rejoined the yard, you will be continually assessed by either a yard assessor or a roving assessor from the schools. You should achieve NVQ level II after approximately eighteen months. You can then go on to take level III and NVQ level IV, which will give you the opportunity to go for positions of greater responsibility.

You still have the option of applying direct to a trainer for a placement, who should register you on the scheme so that you can attend one of the schools. *Horses in Training* is a book published annually and lists the names and addresses of trainers throughout the UK. It is available from book shops and in the reference section of most libraries. *The Sporting Life* and the *Racing Post* have a situations vacant section in their classified columns.

Opportunities for further training are few. Racing is a career that offers promotion only through perseverance and years of experience. However, the Racing Industry Short Course (run by Worcester College of Agriculture) is designed for trainers, assistant trainers and senior yard staff. It offers the technical training needed to meet the changing requirements brought about by scientific research and development. The course also provides instruction on equine husbandry of horses in training, and is aimed at people who are experienced in racing yards and are skilled in matters associated with breaking, riding and training routines, but require more background and technical information.

The Racing Schools

The two racing schools at Newmarket and Doncaster train school-leavers and stable staff. All training for British students is provided free of charge, as the costs are borne by various sources within racing and Government funding. Both the schools take overseas students, with a fee for the service. The racing school in Newmarket is actively involved in developing an EU dimension to its training programme. Unlike the few overseas racing schools, the British racing schools will take girls and boys and teach them all aspects of working with racehorses from mucking out to riding, with a fair share of classroom work. Entry is by way of an interview or recommendation from a trainer. Some riding experience is preferred, but not essential.

The schools are organised along the lines of a real racing stable, with tuition given by experienced instructors, some of whom are ex-professional jockeys. The schools have excellent facilities, including all-weather gallops. The British Racing School at Newmarket also has an indoor school. Both schools have their own horses, many are former racehorses, but there are quieter horses and ponies for complete beginners.

The courses involve early morning work, including grooming, feeding and mucking out, together with practical riding instruction. Later on in the day, there are lectures on various subjects, including parts of the horse, horse's health, taking a horse away racing and many other matters connected with the work of the industry.

At the Northern Racing School, suitable lodgings can be found in the vicinity of the school for trainees from outside the area.

At the British Racing School, accommodation is in a hostel, where trainees will usually find themselves sharing a room with another person. Meals are provided by catering staff, and there are facilities for doing your laundry. For your own benefit, the schools have strict codes of conduct. For example, no-one is allowed to leave the school at any time without permission, but no doubt you will find that you are too tired at the end of each day to even consider going out!

Michelle Appleby, a trainee at the British Racing School, has set her heart on becoming a jockey:

> 'When I was about five or six, my godparents bought me a pony, and that's what got me started. I used to take him on the beach, shorten my stirrups and gallop along the sand. I also used to watch the racing on TV.
>
> 'It's the thrill of racing that appeals to me more than anything else; it is one of the most exciting equestrian sports there is. There's also the element of danger – it's not like an office job where you're sat in a chair nine to five, it's a great physical challenge.
>
> 'My ambition is to be a National Hunt jockey; I doubt I'll make the weight for flat racing. Hopefully, I will make the grade. I should at least get a few rides. If I don't, I'll probably work my way up through the yard to become head lad, then assistant trainer, but right now I can't see myself failing – I'll keep trying till I succeed.'

The most enjoyable aspect of the day for all the students is going up the gallops. Riders jump off in twos or threes and an instructor drives a van alongside, giving advice on their position and helping them get back in control if they get into difficulty – it can be quite frightening to be bolted with, and the instructor will talk you through, so you can regain control. It's a far better system than learning the hard way in a racing yard. Michelle says of the training:

> 'I think I'm doing really well on the course. I've definitely improved all round. My attitude towards my work is good and I'm really enjoying it. The best part is leading the horses back after the canters, having done really well and ridden better than the day before. Knowing you're improving and getting more control in your riding helps get you through the daily work routine. Riding short is very different from riding long, which is why training here is such an asset. Now I can sit on a racehorse and feel quite safe, whereas when I first came here, I felt a bit insecure.
>
> 'On the whole, I find the training really interesting. The worst thing is getting up early in the morning, but it gets easier as you get used to it. I also enjoy the stable management aspect. If you want to work with horses, you've got to be good at looking after them as well as riding them.
>
> 'There's no competition between the students, we all muck in and help each other because we realise that we're all at different levels, and we encourage each other a lot. Sometimes we look up to the better riders and think that one day we're going to be better than them.'

Only a few students get homesick; most are used to being away from home so it doesn't bother them, particularly when they are enjoying the course too much! The instructors are all exceptionally good at their jobs. They tell you where you're going wrong and only shout at you when you need it! 'Some people are more suited to this way of life than others,' believes Michelle. 'We had three people leave here in the first week. I don't think that they could handle the situation.' She sums up her situation thus:

> 'I've heard the wages in the horse industry are quite poor, but at the moment I'm young, single and I don't think that I need that much money. I don't spend much here and I'm surviving pretty well.

> Having had a taste of racing life, I would certainly recommend it to others – if you don't mind hard work, long hours and early starts! It is a very challenging and rewarding career. My ultimate ambition is, like many others, to win the Grand National.'

Once you have completed your training at one of these schools, they will help you to find a placement with a trainer if you want an apprenticeship, or find you a job if you want to be a stable lad.

Apprenticeships

Racing is one of the few sports that makes small men into giants. Not surprisingly, youngsters, particularly boys, come into the industry wanting to be jockeys. The most important criteria for apprentices is weight. In flat racing, the ideal minimum weight for boys under seventeen years is under seven stone. Girls must be under eight stone. The main reason for most apprentices failing to make the grade is that they grow too heavy.

Girls, in particular, find it difficult to keep their weight down. Muscle is heavier than fat, and girls find they require a greater density of muscle to gain the same amount of strength as a man. Consequently, they have to put on more weight to achieve the strength required for stable work and riding strong horses, which is why you see very few women flat race jockeys. There are many extremely talented female work riders in Newmarket, but Mother Nature doesn't do them any favours where weight is concerned. Although there are some very competent lady jockeys in flat and National Hunt racing, most ride on an amateur basis and in Ladies' Races.

There is no formal training scheme for Steeplechase jockeys, many of whom are ex-flat race apprentices who have grown too heavy. However, a form of apprenticeship has been introduced for conditional jockeys between the ages of sixteen and twenty-five, which provides for instruction to be given by the trainer, with a view to race riding if good enough. Apprentices and conditional jockeys are given a weight allowance when riding in races, to compensate for their lack of experience, but these have to be given up when a full jockey's licence is applied for.

Professional Jockey

Most professional jockeys are stable jockeys under contract to one particular trainer. As a stable jockey, your success will depend very much on the trainer you are riding for. You may, of course, be offered rides by other trainers, particularly those who do not have enough horses to employ a stable jockey. Your own trainer will usually give permission for you to ride if he has no rides for you.

The life of a jockey is not all glamour. In flat racing particularly, the constant struggle to keep your weight down is a daily battle of exercise, saunas and strict dieting. There is also the travelling involved: you may be expected to work ride at your trainer's yard in the morning, drive up the motorway to an afternoon meeting, then drive onto an evening meeting across the country. Not all jockeys are privileged enough to have private helicopters, and many rely on their wives or colleagues to drive them from one meeting to another, some suffering greatly from the strain of travelling.

At race meetings, you are expected to show respect to the trainer, his wife and the owners, as well as to racecourse officials, which isn't always easy. Some trainers and owners might treat you like the stable dog – pat you on the head when you do well, but take it out on you when things go wrong, because you're not in a position to retaliate.

It's a tough way of life, governed by rules and officials and the fickle public, who will adore you when you win, and heckle you when you don't. Only a handful of jockeys reach the top. The majority achieve an average amount of rides and wins. So many youngsters only see the glamorous side of a jockey's career, and come into racing wanting to get to the top as jockeys. It is a very rewarding and exciting career, but it is also very dangerous, hard work and full of disappointments. Flat racing offers higher financial rewards and relatively fewer falls than National Hunt, although it is said that National Hunt racing has a closer-knit community with greater camaraderie between jockeys, owners and trainers. To succeed as a jockey, you need to be an exceptionally talented and dedicated rider, with a good trainer and sound family back-up if you are to survive the highs and lows of a riding career.

LIFE IN A RACING YARD

On the whole, racing has done much to get away from the out-dated image of employers who treat their staff in a shabby, uncaring way, but it still has some hurdles to overcome in order to shed that image completely. Together with the racing schools, the RTBTB and the BHB, the Stable Lads Association is striving towards that goal.

If you work in the racing industry and have had poor conditions or unfair or unreasonable work practices, don't let one bad employer put you off. Racing is a wonderful way of life with many opportunities. Work out your notice, as required in your contract of employment (don't simply walk out on a job, it will make it very difficult for you to get accepted in another yard), and look for another trainer who is willing to take you on. Those trainers who treat their employees badly have a reputation that is well known among other trainers and head lads within the industry.

Stable Lads

Stable lads are the backbone of the industry because it is the lads who come into closest contact with the horses. Racehorses are highly strung creatures with complex natures and a multitude of idiosyncracies. Due to the intensity of their training, they can be very fractious and aggressive to handle. A lad who is happy and contented with his or her job and really loves the horses, keeps them sweeter than one who isn't. If you go into racing just for the glamour, you won't last long; you must really love the animals as well as the sport.

Racing stables, unlike many competition yards, often have a routine. Unless you are taking a horse to a race meeting, your day will always start and finish at the same time. A sample day's work is given below:

6 am – Head lad (only) feeds horses and puts up the board for the day's riders.
7 am – Lads arrive on yard, muck out and tack up first lot.
7.30 am – First lot out.
8.30 am – Return, untack, give hay. Breakfast.
9 am – Second lot mucked out and tacked up.
9.30 am – Second lot out.
10.30 am – Ride third lot (which is usually mucked out for you) then clean tack, sweep yard and feed horses.
1 pm – Lunch, then the afternoon is free.
4 pm – Return to yard, muck out, hay and groom your horses (you should have no more than three to do, unless staff are off sick).
5 pm – Trainer's inspection. You will have to 'show' your horses for the trainer, who usually discusses the animal's progress with the head lad. The horses are then fed at 6.30 pm, and you are finished for the evening. In most stables the lads take it in turns to do night stables at about 10 pm,

checking that all the horses are okay, and have enough water.

Looking after racehorses requires a high standard of grooming. You have to be quick and efficient, and be constantly aware of any changes in the horses' health, both physical and psychological. Riding racehorses is very different from riding ordinary horses. Apart from their hour's exercise, they are stabled for twenty-three hours a day and rarely turned out to graze. (National Hunt horses often have a more lenient programme.) After coming up from grass, they are given five to eight weeks' initial road work at walk and trot to get them fit and by the fourth week they are usually jumping out of their skins to canter. Horses in training can become very screwed up; they worry a lot more – not surprising when their environment is so unnatural to them. Some adjust better than others, but it is important for them to have quiet, caring grooms. You can't be loud or aggressive with racehorses – you'll have them climbing the walls, and you'll get nowhere.

Trudy Pearson has worked in racing for twenty-two years, and is now head lad in a top yard. Trudy started her career in racing when it was still unusual for girls to be stable lads:

> 'In the first job I had, I was the only girl in the yard. It was awful to begin with. I think a lot of the lads felt their way of life was under threat by some mythical feminist movement. Having it so tough to begin with has hardened me a lot. It wasn't a top yard: the trainer worked for the training fees rather than the prize money, the emphasis being on bulk rather than quality – he had over eighty horses in training, but most of them were only good for selling races, only a handful were decent.
>
> 'The head lad was one of these old boys who'd been in racing for about fifty years, and he would constantly make sexist remarks, like how women were only good for having babies and cooking. I just used to bite my lip and get on with the job. I learned a hell of a lot from that old guy, though. He was strict but he knew so much about racing and horses. In the end he came to respect the fact that I was a competent work rider and never shirked any of the heavy work.'

Riding ability also plays an important part when working in flat racing. Thoroughbreds are broken in at about eighteen months of age so they can be trained and fit in time for the start of the season in spring. The horses are still physically and mentally immature; some can be quiet and gentle to ride, but as Trudy discovered, some can be down-right wicked:

> 'You have to be a very confident rider and totally indifferent to the antics of the livelier horses, particularly when they are trying to unseat or unnerve you. During the first eight weeks in the yard, I fell off every Monday because the horses were extra fresh from not having been ridden the day before, and from being kept in their stables all the time. It was quite nerve racking at first, but as I got used to it and learned to stay on, the horses realised I wasn't bothered and stopped trying. Also, they were much more quiet when they started canter work.'

During training, most racehorses don't get turned out at all; the only grazing they get is in hand with their lads after exercise or perhaps in the evening for a short time. The style of riding is very different to normal riding: racehorses are given the minimum of schooling to teach them to gallop in a straight line, jump out of the starting stalls and understand the hands, heels and whip.

Trudy continues:

> 'After four years I left the job. The head lad and trainer both gave me a great reference and I got a job with a more successful trainer. There were a few other girls working there, so I had a lot less ribbing. The horses were much better bred and trained and I led up my first winner during my second week there – I'll never forget that. I was more elated about it than the jockey! The trainer and head lad were not nearly so chauvinistic; they were both quite a bit younger than my last bosses and us girls got as much opportunity to ride and look after the good horses, including the colts, as the boys.'

An important part of work with racehorses is accompanying them to meetings, travelling with them in the box and leading them up before and after the race.

Trudy stayed in racing until the birth of her daughter, Ashley. A year later, her old boss offered her the job of head lad.

> 'I jumped at the chance. I missed the work dreadfully and I wasn't going to pass up the chance to earn a decent wage. My duties now involve the day-to-day running of the yard, feeding horses, administering treatment if they're ill, breaking in the yearlings when they arrive in October and supervising the lads in the yard and out riding.

'I don't travel at all, now I'm head lad. Ashley is growing up with racing very much the core of her life – my boss is terrific about time off for illnesses and school plays and he helps with childminding fees. Years ago, women head lads were unheard of. Racing has changed a lot in the past two decades.

'One of my jobs is to recruit staff. My boss is a brilliant trainer but hates anything to do with people, especially when he has to chat up owners! We get a lot of youngsters from the racing schools and it's great to see they are getting some proper training, instead of being plunged in at the deep end. It's still a tough life, so you've got to be resilient enough to take the knocks. However, if you really love the horses and the sport it's a great career.'

FURTHER OPPORTUNITIES

Travelling Lad

So much of racing is centred around travelling horses to meetings that many large yards employ full- and part-time travelling lads. Picked for their reliability and organisational skills, travelling lads have to do more than just drive the lorry. They take the head lad's responsiblilities for the feeding and welfare of the horses and take charge of the lads that accompany them. On non-racing days, they ride out and groom along with the other lads. Most travelling lads are stable lads or work riders who have taken their HGV driving tests especially to do this job.

Horsebox driver

Some of the larger racing stables prefer to employ someone whose sole duty is to drive the box, with a travelling lad supervising the other lads and horses. For this, you may need some knowledge of handling horses, but more importantly, you will need to have a clean, current HGV licence. Driver's jobs are advertised in the equestrian and racing press.

Assistant Trainer

If you're blessed with the right connections in racing, or have proved yourself talented and dedicated enough as a stable lad, you could be promoted to assistant trainer. Many yards have more horses in training than one trainer can cope with, so as his or her right-hand man, you will be doing exactly the same job; in particular, accompanying the horses to race meetings to saddle up the horses, entertain the owners and pass on instructions to the jockey.

It is a more lucrative job than that of head lad, and you will need to prove that you are capable of recognising a horse's potential, its level of fitness and the ground conditions and distance at which it is best suited to race. You will also be required to assist with race entry forms, public relations, recruiting and training stable staff – in short, all the jobs a trainer hates, but loves to delegate!

Trainer

Successful trainers tend to be former jockeys, or assistant trainers who have built up the necessary finances and a good reputation within the industry. To set up and profitably run a racing yard requires not only a knowledge of horses, but good contacts both within the industry and throughout the business world.

Racehorse owners are a trainer's bread and butter. You must be capable of persuading people to invest in a horse, then find them a good one and train that horse to win races. People like to own racehorses for a number of reasons: a love of racing, the social attraction of racecourses, providing a relaxing and alluring setting to entertain business clients, the tax concessions now available when owning a racehorse and the profits and accolades bestowed upon you if it turns out to be a winner.

It is not as easy and glamorous a job as it looks. Of course, there is the prestige attached to being a successful trainer and fame and fortune to be achieved. Behind the scenes, however, a lot of hard work goes into the consistent production and turnover of good horses.

Jack Wilson has been training horses in flat racing for six years:

> 'I had no previous experience with horses before getting into racing. I worked my way up through the ranks, starting off as an apprentice – which I soon got too heavy for – stable lad, head lad and finally assistant trainer.
>
> 'I took over this yard when the previous trainer retired. It's not been as easy as it sounds. In order to take on this yard, I've had to do a lot of crawling to the bank and to my family. You need more than financial back-up to run a yard. My wife does all my secretarial

work, as well as riding out when staff are on holiday or away racing.'

As a trainer, you have to be up early; there's no rest even for the top people in any type of racing yard. Jack is up by seven to put out the list of exercise lots for the day:

'By the time first lot pulls out at seven-thirty, I'm up on the gallops with my head lad, Peter, to watch the horses working. We discuss each animal's progress and where and when we should race him. After the first lot, we return for breakfast, and then we discuss the horses some more – it's horses for breakfast, dinner and lunch in racing stables, and it's no different whether you're the stable lad, the jockey or trainer. If I can, I go out and watch second and third lot, unless I have to travel to a meeting, in which case I leave the horses to Peter, and get changed to go racing. During the season, I'm rarely at home for the morning work, but by then the horses are fit and ready and I can work out their racing schedules for the rest of the season on how they fare on the track.

'Before a race, I saddle up the horse and brief the jockey. If it is his first time on the animal, he'll usually ask the lad what the horse like to ride; it's one thing watching a horse from the ground, but quite another to be in the plate. Most of the time the horse's owners are there, and once the horse is on his way down to the start, I take the owners back to the stands to watch the race. If I think the horse has a good chance I'll say so, but if the opposition looks good on form and from inside knowledge, I'll tell the owners and leave the choice of whether to place a bet up to them.

'Most of my owners have only two or three horses in training; I don't want to make the mistake of putting all my eggs in one basket. During the start of the 1990 recession, a lot of trainers went bankrupt, particularly as a result of Middle Eastern owners pulling out of the British racing industry following the Gulf War. Despite all the yards that have closed, the industry is recovering, albeit slowly.'

For anyone wanting to train horses, whether it be flat or National Hunt, it's not impossible, but it is a long, hard slog to the top, and even harder to stay there. If you cannot take over an established yard, you may be able to start up by training your own horses, and if they are successful, you may find owners for them, as well as others who are prepared to send their horses to you.

STUD WORK

The Thoroughbred breeding industry plays a major part in the breeding and export of horses in Britain. The general principle of breeding horses is, 'to put the best to the best, and hope for the best'. Studs can be divided into two main categories: public studs – which 'stand' stallions (the majority of which also own broodmares); and private studs – which own or keep broodmares.

Training for Stud Work

Opened in 1967, the National Stud in Newmarket is a Government-owned, public establishment where half a dozen good commercial stallions stand, and there are a few mares there privately owned.

Every year, around 150 young men and women apply for places on the National Stud's training course – and only fifteen are accepted. The selection procedure is rigorous, although academic qualifications are not the most important factor; the students who are accepted are the ones who impress at the interview with a genuine interest and desire to succeed. However, experience of working with horses (though not necessarily breeding stock) is the one essential qualification.

The idea of the course is to train young people to a level where they can take a responsible job. Training at the stud is run along the lines of the work routine in most studs. Students are required to work for the breeding season – February 15 to July 15. During those six months, you will live in a hostel on-site and are paid a gross wage of around £80 per week. You are expected to be available for work seven days a week, but occasionally days off are allowed, depending on the workload. Practical experience in the environment of a busy public stud is an important part of the course and during the season students will work in each of the units on the stud. You will have a spell in the ten different yards at the stud – the foaling unit, nursery yards, isolation yard, etc., where you work under a yard foreman. Time is also spent in the stallion unit, but you will not be required to handle the stallions. Duties include mucking out, assisting the vet, teasing, general care of mares and foals, stud maintenance, office work and assisting with the public tours of the stud.

Besides the practical experience, you will also attend a wide range of lectures – fifty in all, given by leading authorities in stud management, veterinary medicine, first aid, feeding, pedigrees, pasture management and other related subjects. These are also open to employees or trainees at other studs in the Newmarket area, for a fee. Students are also taken on a number of outside visits to see studs, training yards, veterinary centres and other related activities. At the end of the course there is a written examination which accounts for 40% of your final marks, with on-going assessment providing a further 40%, and a formal end-of-course interview, 20%. The pass rate is high, and the stud's Diploma is highly regarded in the industry as a reference of merit. For further information contact the Assistant Manager at the National Stud.

Further Opportunities

Stud workers are paid according to experience, but as a guide, wages are rather higher than the minimum agricultural wage. Opportunities for promotion in stud work are fairly limited, but the positions of stallion men or stud grooms carry better salaries for added responsibilities.

Once you have recognised qualifications and experience of working in the British Thoroughbred industry, you are assured of a welcome in high-class establishments around the globe where you can work under excellent conditions, carrying responsibility for horses worth millions, and take home an enviable salary. Further advice on careers in stud work can be obtained from the Thoroughbred Breeders Association, including a list of TBA members/studs willing to take working pupils as trainees.

Bloodstock Agencies

A bloodstock agent's job brief is quite wide ranging. It goes from arranging matings and researching the breeding and racing potential of horses, to buying horses at sales and privately on behalf of people who want to breed or race them.

There are no academic qualifications required for this career, although a sound knowledge of Thoroughbred breeding and conformation is essential. For this reason, the majority of people who work for bloodstock agencies start off at the bottom, working as a stable lad in a racing yard or stud assistant in a Thoroughbred stud, then work up through the ranks, gaining knowledge and proving their worth as good judges of horses, with a sound knowledge of the breeding and racing history of Thoroughbreds. You will require a numerical mind; a lot of the work involves figures and computer skills are also essential. You need to be a good communicator, as the bulk of your work involves dealing with people – breeders, buyers and sellers.

Suitable training could involve a specialist degree such as the honours degree in Equine Studies at Warwickshire College – the college which has pioneered so much of Britain's equine education. This degree includes an optional racing module.

Bloodstock agency is a good career which offers a high salary, often on a commission basis, and plenty of opportunity for overseas travel, particularly to places like Ireland, France and the Middle East, which has strong ties with the British racing industry. Vacancies with agencies can be found in the racing press, and also by word of mouth.

RACECOURSE AND TECHNICAL WORK

Very few racecourses employ more than a handful of people and jobs as racecourse managers or clerks of the course seldom become available. However, there are opportunities for carpenters, electricians and painters on some of the bigger courses. The Racecourse Association at Ascot can sometimes help with advice and any vacancies.

Security Work

Financed by the Horserace Betting Levy Board, racing's security is provided by the Jockey Club Security Department. They supply security supervisors, ring inspectors and betting intelligence officers, mainly former police officers, to work on racecourses. Laboratory staff to handle dope tests are employed by Horseracing Forensic Laboratory Limited in Newmarket, Suffolk.

Administration, Clerical and Secretarial Work

All the organisations and associations connected to racing have a limited number of secretarial opportunities. Your best chance of secretarial employment within the industry is with the trainers. Book-keeping skills including wages, VAT and PAYE, and a knowledge of the system of entering and declaring horses for races are essential requirements. Audio-typing, or using shorthand with copy-typing are also useful. Word-processing skills and computer knowledge are also a considerable advantage. Suitable training could be found on one of the specialist college courses at Warwick or Witney. The National Trainers' Federation can sometimes help with vacancies for trainer's secretaries. If you want to combine secretarial work with riding, you can often find a trainer who is looking for both a secretary and work rider. It is a nice combination, offering fresh air and exercise and often, with a better wage than that of ordinary grooms or secretaries.

Racing Journalism

Like all aspects of journalism, this is one of the hardest fields to break into, with applicants far outnumbering vacancies. You will need basic training in journalism, either through college or with a local newspaper. Most racing journalists have first worked with national newspapers. Some, in particular television journalists, are ex-jockeys with a flair for commentary and an invaluable familiarity with the sport and its characters, both equine and human. *The Sporting Life* and the *Racing Post* are the only two racing dailies, but most national and some regional newspapers include racing in their sports section. The training required to be an equestrian journalist is covered in the section on associated trades (see Chapter Three – Further Opportunities).

The Racing Employment Register

This register was established at the Jockey Club in 1992. It is run on a database system, providing employers looking for staff with a list of people from the industry with appropriate experience, who are currently out of work. If you have been made redundant, or are unable to continue in an existing job, perhaps for health reasons, the register will enable you to find appropriate employment in another part of the industry. However, the concept is not designed to help those currently in work to find a different job in racing. Both employers and those without a job should apply in writing to the Jockey Club for the appropriate form.

Whatever aspect of work you do in racing, you will require perseverance, dedication and hard work; in return, you can expect a great deal of career satisfaction with decent wages. Working directly with the horses offers a unique and healthy way of life. Only a lucky few who succeed as jockeys or trainers will achieve fame and fortune, but there are so many other interesting and financially rewarding careers within the industry, making it a worthwhile vocation .

Chapter 5

The Field of Medicine

OPPORTUNITIES IN VETERINARY CARE

Those dedicated to the medical care and well-being of horses are the unsung heroes of the horse industry. Veterinary work is similar to groom's work, in that it involves long, unsociable hours, although of course, most veterinary work is better paid. Becoming a veterinary surgeon, nurse or animal therapist involves both practical and academic talents. Have you always been interested in the mechanics of how animals work and do you have compassion for the suffering? It isn't enough just to like the idea of becoming a vet, or nurse, or chiropractic – you must be firmly committed and dedicated to the work because there is a long, hard road ahead of you. Training to be a veterinary surgeon takes up to six years, then it is a long haul to build up a successful practice.

The opportunities to specialise in the medical care of the horse are growing. Veterinary surgeons have the chance to take further training in equine studies, equine stud management and equine orthopaedics. Veterinary nurses who also have experience in handling horses will find themselves at an advantage when applying for jobs at practices that have a large number of horses on their books.

Natural healing arts are growing in the field of animal medicine. Vets can take courses in homeopathy, and the School of McTimoney Chiropractic will take on students who can prove they have a natural aptitude towards healing. Another sphere that doesn't involve academic training, but does require a lot of practical ability and knowledge is horse dentistry, although Britain does not have an official training scheme for this worthwhile vocation.

Veterinary Nursing

The working life of a veterinary nurse encompasses a wide variety of tasks. For example, duties include reception work, receiving the patients and their owners. You are the 'bridge' between the vet and his clients, so a good manner is essential. You will be doing general administration, such as filing case records, keeping accounts, dealing with telephone enquiries and answering routine questions. You need to be good at organising, be numerate and possess good communication skills.

On the veterinary side, you will be responsible for the care and maintenance of equipment, cleaning and preparing the operating theatre, sterilising instruments, and making sure that everything is in good working order. High standards are important. You will assist with operations, handing instruments to the vet and helping with anaesthetics under supervision. You will also have to assist with humanely destroying animals if they are very ill or unwanted.

The work also involves looking after the needs of in-patients, feeding, cleaning and exercising animals, and doing things like changing dressings and removing stitches. On the technical side, you will produce X-ray photographs and carry out laboratory tests on urine, blood, faeces and other samples.

Most veterinary nurses work in small animal practices (with domestic pets) but some work with large (horses or farm) animals, in zoos, research departments and clinics, for pharmaceutical companies, or for animal charities. In veterinary nursing, the pay won't be brilliant, and unlike groom's work, you won't have 'perks' to help improve your lifestyle. You must be interested in animals without being too sentimental, and not squeamish when it comes to operations and putting animals to sleep. You also have to be good with people; owners can be more difficult to handle than their pets!

Your hours will include working weekends and evenings to cover surgery times, but if you have a genuine desire to care for animals, job satisfaction is high. You can work as an unqualified animal nurse, in which case you would be trained by the vets you work for, or you can become qualified through the Veterinary Nurse Training Scheme. You will then be called a veterinary nurse, accredited by the Royal College of Veterinary Surgeons.

To apply for this scheme you must be aged seventeen or over, and have your parents' consent if you are under eighteen. You must be gainfully employed at an approved training centre for a minimum of thirty-five hours per week, or have written promise of such employment. Finally, you must have at least four GCSEs, minimum grade C. Subjects must include English language and either a physical or biological science or mathematics (subjects like physics and chemistry are physical sciences). Although the entry requirement is four GCSEs, qualified veterinary nurse, Dawn McHugh BHSPI, believes that you really need six:

'Students have to be relatively bright to pass the veterinary nursing exams. The ones who come in on four GCSEs struggle. When I examine veterinary nurses, I find the ones with basic exam passes do very badly. There is a high failure rate, of about fifty per cent.'

When it comes to training and employment in veterinary nursing, there are many parallels between this profession and groom's work. Dawn McHugh, who is head nurse at the Animal Health Clinic in Newmarket, stresses that determination and initiative are also essential qualities:

'Anyone who is just going to be brow-beaten by unscrupulous employers, who are going to keep them in a little practice and not allow them to do very much, will not be very happy. Whereas, if you've got enough initiative to know that is not what you want, and that you are qualified to do very much more, then you are going to go out looking for something better. There are plenty of jobs in veterinary practices that will enable you to use your skills to the full.'

There is also an advanced diploma that you can take, and Dawn was one of the first people to study for one:

'It carries with it no extra flags. It doesn't give you the right to do anything more than you did before, but what will undoubtedly happen is that the better jobs, for example, head nursing, will go to holders of this diploma. There is no other opportunity for further training.'

You can train anywhere in the country. Most veterinary practices are approved training centres for nurses.

'The training involves going on either a full- or part-time course, or studying "in-house",' explains Dawn. 'But it's cheaper to get trainees than to take on qualified nurses, so many practices take on several trainees and don't train them well, and consequently the students get dissatisfied and lose interest.

'As in groom's work, it's easy to end up on that road. You have to be very ambitious and make sure you steer yourself in the right direction. It depends on whether you think it's all going to be puppies and kittens to cuddle or whether it's going to be a profession.'

Typically, hours are between thirty-five and forty a week, and also time being on-call, that is, getting called in for emergencies or doing phone duty in the evenings. A lot of practices provide accommodation on site, which is fine initially, but that situation does have strings attached – like being put on telephone duty, or called out at all hours of the day and night because you happen to be handy!

'Pay varies considerably,' warns Dawn McHugh. 'Because practices take you on as a trainee, the pay is poor initially, but it's still better than trainee groom's pay. Pay doesn't necessarily increase a great deal on qualifying. Veterinary nursing has no statutory minimum wage, which is a big problem – there's always someone willing who will work for less!'

For the seriously ambitious, there are opportunities for diversification. Some agricultural colleges teach veterinary nursing, including lecturing and full-time courses, so there may be teaching jobs available. 'Repping' (becoming a sales representative) is another big area, explains Dawn:

> 'Pharmaceutical companies find veterinary nurses are extremely good at selling their products, because most of them have been on the buying end. Also the veterinary profession seems much more willing to listen to veterinary nurses than they do to a typical rep. Nurses have been very successful at selling and from there, a considerable number have gone into management within their companies. It's very much a career change and an opportunity to move on from the original qualification. Many nurses have also gone into marketing, which pays well. Companies value first-hand experience in caring for animals.
>
> 'More and more equine practices are beginning to take qualified veterinary nurses. The problem there, though, is that not all nurses are horsey. I think you've got to be horsey to be employed by an equine practice, because nobody is going to take you on, no matter how good a nurse you are, if you can't hang onto a loopy horse! A lot of nurses who have their own horses and ride take those sort of positions.
>
> 'The integration of Britain in the European Union also adds to prospects. Many nurses are going abroad. Our qualifications are very highly thought of around the world. You can go out to the United States or Europe. The wages, conditions and prospects abroad are often very much better. In the end, it's up to you to make your own success.'

Having kept horses all her life, Dawn has always been interested in veterinary work:

'When I was looking around for jobs I contacted the Vet's School at Cambridge University to do work experience. I thought I was going to work in the yard and found myself working in the kennels, which absolutely horrified me because I spent most of the day cleaning out kennels! But I stuck at it.

'Veterinary nurse training is small animal, it doesn't involve any horses at all. But it may be that the practice in which you train does some horse work. The practice I worked at had an equine side to it as well, but the training is purely small animal and having got into it, I found I didn't miss the horses at all.

'I stayed in nursing and did the BHS training on a part-time basis in my spare time! I didn't go on any courses. After I qualified as a nurse at twenty, I passed my BHSPI a year later. At the time, I had some vague idea about going into teaching. But surgery is where my heart is. It's strange, but when I started nursing the one place I said I did not want to work was in theatre. Now I'm head nurse and theatre superintendent at one of the best animal clinics in the country!

'I've only been here three years, and my purpose when I came was to set up a nursing team, which I'm in the middle of doing, so I'd like to see that through. I like clinical work; I work mainly in the theatre and can't imagine not being involved with horses on their backs! I'm not sure where I want to go from here. I do quite a lot of public speaking for nurses, which I enjoy, but at present I don't think I could have anything better than what I've got at the moment.

'If you want to do horse veterinary work, be aware that it is a very small sphere. I'm in a very privileged position here because I do both equine and small animal, but I'm doing it in the best place I could. These jobs are very few and far between, so if you are interested, you've got to be prepared to do small animal work initially.'

Veterinary Surgery

One of the first lessons you learn when you own or work with horses is that you have two very important allies, one is your farrier, who takes care of your horse's shoeing needs, and the other is your vet, who cares for your horse's medical needs.

There are over eleven thousand qualified vets on the register of the Royal College of Veterinary Surgeons, the governing body for the profession. Veterinary work is open to both men and women, although at present, there are more male than female vets (amongst students, there are more women than men). Some aspects of veterinary work can be physically demanding, but it is found that women vets generally cope without difficulty with large animals, such as horses.

Where physical disabilities are concerned, it is always a case of individual capabilities. One veterinary school trained a deaf student, a colour blind student, and a student unable to walk unaided, all of whom graduated successfully. Some types of veterinary work, like research, are suitable for people with mobility problems.

Qualifications and training

The only way to qualify as a vet is to take a veterinary degree at one of six universities – Bristol, Cambridge, Edinburgh, Glasgow, Liverpool and London (the Royal Veterinary College). The courses last five years (six at Cambridge) and entry is very competitive. More than eighty per cent of applicants are turned down. Mature students are very unlikely to be accepted if over thirty years old. Graduates who already have a degree in another subject can be accepted, but may have considerable difficulty in financing themselves through the long course, as they will not be eligible for a second mandatory grant from their local authority.

To work as a vet you have to be academic, as well as practical. Very high grades are required at both GCSE (or equivalent) and at A level. The GCSEs are very important, because they are the only exams which most applicants have actually taken when they complete their application forms. Selectors generally look for at least six or seven grade As!

At A level (or equivalent), two grade As and one grade B is the minimum likely to be required (three grade As for Cambridge). Chemistry or physical science must be offered at A level (or perhaps AS level). The requirement for other subjects varies a little from university to university, but you should have two from maths, physics, and biology or zoology. Some universities insist on a biological subject, and feel that students without biology are at a disadvantage. You must check the requirements very carefully in the university prospectuses. Also, the more university requirements you meet, the wider the choice you will have when applying for a post.

During training, the subjects include: anatomy, embryology, physiology, biochemistry, animal husbandry, animal behaviour, pathology, immunology, pharmacology, virology, bacteriology, parasitology and toxicology. With all these 'ology's to learn, you've got to be very bright and willing to work hard, if you're going to succeed. Medicine and surgery are studied in depth. For practical veterinary experience, the schools include a period of six months in practice during vacations.

There are some differences in emphasis in the various courses, arising from the nature of the areas in which the schools are located. There is an 'east-west divide', with Glasgow, Liverpool and Bristol offering experience with a fair mix of animals, from small domestic pets to horses, and Cambridge and Edinburgh offering rather less horse and dairy farming contact. You should look into course differences carefully, before completing your university application form.

Get some experience before you leave school. Ring your local vet or veterinary hospital and ask if you can do some work experience, perhaps over the school holidays. Try to persuade one of the vets to let you accompany him or her on a day's rounds, and to observe what goes on in the surgery. If you're really keen, the vet may let you help out at weekends and in the holidays. Any previous experience of coping with animals will be invaluable in helping you get a place at university.

Personal qualities

It takes more than obvious academic ability to be a successful vet, the right sort of personality and attitudes are essential in keeping your clients; you will have a lot of competition, from within your own practice and from other practices. Veterinary surgeon David Buckley, BVetMed, CertESM, MRCVS, explains what it takes to succeed:

> 'The qualities needed to go into veterinary work are initially, a very heavy scientific background. Until you're almost in your last year of training, you will have nothing to do with the living animal – it is all to do with learning anatomy, physiology, biochemistry and pathology. Eventually, however, you will get to put it together and see the live animal, but that's not a very great percentage of the course; most of it is scientific ability. The skill to absorb a large amount of facts is vitally important in training.
>
> 'The practical side is something which, unfortunately, because of the heavy emphasis on the scientific ability, has to an extent, somewhat been forgotten. Because of the pressure on the number of places available, there had been a bias shown to the scientifically able students. Thankfully, policy has changed and there is now a move back to an interviewing system, where students are interviewed personally before being offered a place, to find the more practical sort of person, who's good at handling animals as well as knowing the mechanics of them.'

Once you have graduated, there are opportunities to specialise in equine medicine. The certificates in Equine Practice, Equine Orthopaedics and Equine Stud Medicine are available to those who have been graduates for at least three calendar years, and who have spent at least two calendar years in veterinary work which has included a reasonable element of equine practice, equine orthopaedics or equine stud medicine, as appropriate. Therefore you will need to join a veterinary practice that specialises in your chosen field as an assistant vet to get a thorough grounding of the knowledge and experience you will need.

You can also go on to diploma level in Equine Stud Medicine and Equine Orthopaedics. There is no diploma examination in Equine Practice. If you want to know more about these certificates and diplomas, contact the Royal College of Veterinary Surgeons.

If you want to specialise in equine medicine, you cannot afford to take time out to work with horses. You could, however, take a holiday job between school terms when studying for GCSEs and A levels. This will help achieve your ultimate aim.

Based at the Mullacot Veterinary Hospital in North Devon, David Buckley has concentrated his skills on the reproduction of the horse:

> 'Since my basic five-year training, I've studied for the Certificate in Equine Stud Medicine, my main interest being in the reproduction of the horse. That was a two-year specialisation course. I qualified for that and now I'm working for the Diploma in Equine Stud Medicine, the next stage on.
>
> 'For those wishing to specialise in horses once qualified as a vet, there are other certificates that you can work towards, as well as the equine ones, which if you are working in an equine practice, are very useful to have. For example, an advanced qualification certificate or diploma in anaesthesia or radiography aren't specific to the horse when you take them, but you can go on to develop your own skill in the horse field.'

One of your jobs as a vet will be to keep an eye out for abuse and cruelty. Even less pleasant, but equally important, will be 'euthanasia'. While you are practising in general, you may have to assist in the large scale slaughter of animals, if for instance, there is an outbreak of foot and mouth disease. You have to be objective about animals; if you're too sentimental you won't make a very good vet.

Working in a veterinary surgery involves advising on the general health, care and breeding of animals. In towns and cities, work is almost exclusively with small domestic animals. In more rural areas, most practices are mainly concerned with farm livestock and horses, although some also deal with small domestic animals.

General practice is often very hard work, with long and irregular hours. Although the total work load is usually shared with one or more partners and assistants, there is still a lot of night and weekend work. Emergencies can happen at any time of the day or night, and mares don't foal to order! For rural vets, a lot of travelling is involved getting from one case to the next, and always in a hurry! To be a vet in general practice, you must also be good at running a business, as well as skilled in animal treatment. There are no standard fees for veterinary treatments, so you have to be capable of working out costings and charge reasonable rates for your customers, if you are to keep them. While veterinary work is reasonably secure, it too is dependent on fluctuations in the agricultural and horse economy and the state of people's purses generally. These factors can affect the financial health of a practice.

Most vets entering private practice start as salaried junior assistants working in an established practice, with one or more senior vets. If you want to buy into a practice, it will take some time to accumulate the capital.

Veterinary hospitals

'With the growing number of hospitals that are both small animal and equine, there is an increasing amount of scope for people who want to specialise in horse veterinary work,' explains David Buckley. 'Our practice comes into that category, and we get quite a cross-section of patients. Most of the horses that come here for treatment are privately owned hacks, hunters and a number of racehorses.

'We are regularly inspected by the ruling body of the Royal College of Veterinary Surgeons, and they ensure that our facilities and methods of work are up to a high standard.'

Other Opportunities

A third of all vets do not work from a surgery. One advantage of posts outside general practice is that they usually entail far more regular working hours. They also offer greater financial security, without the stress of running a business. However, vets who go on to more senior posts are likely to find that their work involves little actual contact with animals.

Vets in the horse industry are likely to be employed by companies to research into new drugs or foods.

Some vets are responsible for the welfare of competition animals during transportation. You may choose to specialise in research – for example, in Government laboratories, or university veterinary science departments, where you would also teach veterinary students. Some openings are available working for the Army Veterinary Corps, zoos and other organisations, including overseas posts. You may find yourself working as a racehorse vet in Saudi Arabia, a stud vet in Austria or a rescue vet in Egypt – the possibilities are endless.

ALTERNATIVE THERAPY

The last decade has seen a resurgence in the popularity of natural medicines. For example, there is a homeopathy course at the Faculty of Homeopathy in London, available to qualified veterinary surgeons. Although some vets are sceptical as to the effectiveness of alternative treatment, many animals (and people) have been cured by natural medicines after being 'written off' by a vet (or doctor). Regarding alternative medicines, such as homeopathy, many in the profession prefer to keep an open mind.

'At the hospital we frequently look at new topics to research. Unfortunately, any sort of research is extremely expensive which is why it goes on very slowly,' explains David Buckley. 'To prove something beyond all reasonable doubt is a difficult task. You have to set up controls, either animals or situations which are exactly the same, treated at the same time, under the same weather conditions, nutritional conditions, even under the same work conditions so that the animals have identical treatments. Absolutely the only difference should be that one is receiving homeopathic treatment and the other isn't. With large animals, that is an almost impossible situation to achieve to get accurate results.'

Homeopathy is a form of therapeutics first described by a German physician, Samuel Hahnemann (1755-1843). Being dissatisfied with the medicine of his day, which he came to regard as both dangerous and ineffective, Hahnemann was led by a chance observation to investigate the effects of various medicinal substances, first on himself and subsequently on other healthy volunteers. After six years of experimentation and reflection, he proclaimed a therapeutic principle; namely, that the right way to treat a disease is to give the patient a drug which, if taken by a healthy person, would reproduce the symptoms from which the patient was suffering. For example, the symptoms of Belladonna poisoning resemble the clinical picture of scarlet fever; hence Belladonna is 'homeopathic' to scarlet fever, and may be used to treat it. Hahnemann propounded his theory in the Latin phrase *similia similibus curentur* (let like be cured by like), the Similimum principle. Hahnemann's work is the basis of the homeopathic medicines in use today.

The Faculty of Homeopathy at The Royal London Homeopathic Hospital is the body authorised by Act of Parliament to train medically qualified doctors, veterinary surgeons and dental surgeons in homeopathic medicines. The courses are not open to laymen, although many do practice homeopathy.

The law on treating animals is very strict. You can set up as a homeopathic therapist for humans, but you cannot prescribe medicine to animals unless you are a qualified vet. However, if you have a real interest in homeopathy and have taken an animal course (usually only available on completion of the human course) at one of several centres throughout the UK, you can treat an animal that has been referred to you by a vet. No-one can come directly to you for treatment; it must only be through a vet's referral, otherwise you are breaking the law. This law applies to all alternative carers such as chiropractors, physiotherapists and horse dentists.

McTimoney Chiropractic

Around the time that Xenophon was writing about the art of riding and training horses, Hippocrates, the father of medicine, was emphasising the importance of the spine in relation to health. 'Acquire knowledge of the spine,' he wrote, 'for this is the requisite to understanding many diseases.' It is on the basis of Hippocrates' studies that chiropractic is built.

Today, the horse industry is vastly indebted to the skills of McTimoney Chiropractors. The career of many a champion racehorse or eventer has been saved by the practice of this ancient art.

During your direct work with horses you will most likely witness, and experience when riding, the healing skills of a McTimoney chiropractor. If you have developed a true desire to work in the healing arts, this is one of the most rewarding and challenging careers you could have.

To be a successful chiropractor you must, however, also have a desire to heal humans. If you don't complete and pass the four-year human course, you will not be allowed to take the eighteen-month animal course.

You must be as interested in healing people as animals. Both are equally rewarding.

One quality you will need is sensitivity. The development of the student's palpation and analysis skills in a very gentle and sensitive way are the basic principles upon which the technique is taught. While this skill is developed during your training, an innate talent is helpful.

Good communication skills are also essential. Chiropractic is not a science – it's very controversial – and it is still debatable how it actually works on horses, but the fact that it does work is undeniable. You must gain people's confidence and trust by explaining exactly what you are doing and why, and what will be the desired end. You need a lot of self-confidence to explain to your patient, or owner if it is an animal, what your diagnosis is and your intended course of treatment. Often people will contact a chiropractor through recommendation by a friend or vet, but they may be sceptical about success. It is up to you to build a good reputation.

Training

The Institute of Pure Chiropractic is the professional regulatory body of McTimoney Chiropractors. In 1972, John McTimoney founded the Oxfordshire School of Chiropractic to train a limited number of students in the McTimoney Technique. Study involves a four-year part-time human course and a further eighteen-month animal course.

The courses begin in January each year. The final date for applications is September of the previous year. The fees are quite high. Grants are generally not available, and students are expected to make their own arrangements for funding their place on the course. The School has agreed a loan scheme with the National Westminster Bank, whereby suitable students who can provide a guarantor may be loaned fees that can be repaid out of income after qualification. Those using this scheme will be expected to find a portion of the fees themselves. The McTimoney Chiropractic School Trust is a registered charity and has a Student Hardship Fund which can be used by students who fall into financial hardship while they are on the course. Funds from this source are generally only available to students in the third or fourth year of their course. Repayment is usually over a period of two years from the date of qualifying as a chiropractor.

While the minimum age of entry is eighteen years, applications are preferred from more mature students. The average age of students is thirty-five, and it is unusual for students under twenty-three years of age to be accepted. Candidates should hold two A level passes, including a science subject. They should also have passes in five GCSE subjects, including English and a science subject. Candidates are assessed for their sense of vocation, motivation and qualities of determination and aspiration. The School will generally look favourably on candidates who have acquired practical 'hands-on' experience of other compatible therapies, such as remedial massage.

The study for McTimoney chiropractic requires that students have the facility and the ability to study at home. You will be required to purchase certain equipment and textbooks costing about £600.

Training involves attendance at the School in Oxford for one weekend day per month. The intensive weekend tutorials involve lectures, talks, and practical instruction, together with regular tests and examinations. Students find that they need to study at home for approximately twenty hours per week, in addition to daily practice of chiropractic exercises and attendance at the monthly tutorials. From the second year, students are required to spend several days per year in various regional student training clinics to get hands-on experience and refine their technique. The School plans to introduce annual summer schools of two separate weeks' full-time duration at a university campus. During these intensive summer schools, students will do analytical and laboratory work.

On completion of the four-year training, and after satisfactory examination in all subjects, students are awarded a certificate as a Chiropractic Practitioner and are entitled to use the suffix MC (McTimoney Chiropractor). Qualification by the School to treat humans does not constitute qualification to treat animals. After the eighteen-month animal course, and on successful examination, the suffix AMC (Animal McTimoney Chiropractor) can then be used. Practitioners are registered and licensed annually by the Institute and are required to recognise its strict code of practice.

There are McTimoney chiropractors in some thirty-six English, Welsh and Scottish counties, though sadly, not yet in all parts of the country. The eventual aim is to make McTimoney Chiropractic available throughout the UK.

Sarah Kendal, CPAIPC, a former work rider in racing, is now a qualified McTimoney practitioner:

> 'After finishing school at seventeen, I did a secretarial course so I would have some other kind of skill, before working with horses. After the course, I went straight into racing, starting in a small local

yard. After a while, I realised I wasn't going to get anywhere in the UK. The wages and conditions are so much better abroad, so I went to work in the States and found a job on a racehorse farm for the six-month duration of my work permit. I returned home and I worked locally for a short time, then I went to another racing yard in Ireland for two years. There I met Ronnie Longford, a very successful chiropractor. He was amazing. After examining and treating the horses he would say things like, "Does this one hang to the left?" or, "When you gallop this one, does it go on this lead?" Watching him work, and seeing the results he got made me decide then that being a chiropractor was what I was looking for!

'I came back to the UK and started the course. It is not based on full-time study, so this enabled me to work for racehorse trainer Jimmy Fitzgerald. It was hard work, to do a full-time job and to do the work for the course. I got about two thirds of the way through and I found I was struggling. I stopped working full-time, came home, and took part-time work riding out in the mornings.

'I really enjoyed the course; at the start I didn't particularly want to treat people, but I've enjoyed treating them as much as horses. On the human side, once you learn the treatment techniques you will spend two years in a clinic where you have to treat people with back problems under the supervision of a practitioner. I went to various clinics around the country to see how different practitioners work.

'The training for animal chiropractic involves learning the whole structure of various animals, mainly the horse and dog. Then you go onto differential diagnosis, which is looking for things like lameness. It's important not to miss the obvious – you shouldn't be called in to treat a back problem when it is something like mud fever.

'On the course you will have days away doing lectures, and other days when you go round various yards to get lots of hands-on experience. It's very rewarding work, to treat a horse whose owner has almost given up hope, and when it's better and they're back out hunting or racing, it's nice to see the owner is really happy with him again.

'Once the course is completed and you qualify, you still aren't going to have an immediate practice. It takes six years from when you start a course to get back to where you originally started, building up a name for yourself in a new career – it takes time. I continued to work part-time for about eighteen months, but now I've got enough business not to have to work for anybody else.

> 'I still ride. I don't think you ever lose the buzz of riding and of having a horse, but I have to be careful not to overdo it and damage my hands. It's extremely important to look after them as the work I do is based on their sensitivity.
>
> 'For the future, I would like to develop my skills further on the human side and also to learn other alternative medicine such as acupuncture and homeopathy. Animals respond remarkably well to alternative treatment. Now that I'm qualified and practising full-time, I feel the time and money spent on the training has been well worth it.'

Physiotherapy

Physiotherapy as practised by chartered physiotherapists, is the physical treatment of bone, joint, muscle or nerve problems by means of electrotherapy, mobilisations, massage and exercise. Most physiotherapists also specialise in manipulation, sports injuries and/or stroke rehabilitation, and prospective patients should enquire as to the specialities of the physiotherapist concerned. The aim of the physiotherapist is to use a combination of skills to cure problems and prevent recurrence. In the case of chronic degenerative illness, the aim is to alleviate symptoms and advise on future management. Chartered physiotherapist Ann Longden, MCSP, explains the qualities needed for physiotherapy:

> 'To train for physiotherapy, you must be academic. I think that is unfortunate, because these days we're losing the sort of person who has practical skills. I'm very concerned that we're getting highly academic physiotherapists who can't treat a patient. Basically, the qualifications to get into physio school now are probably higher than medical school, because the competition is so great.
>
> 'Having lectured in physiotherapy, I find the training is extremely intense, with far more examinations than people realise, both on the practical and theoretical level, and it can be a three- or four-year course.'

Most colleges do a three-year degree course, others do four years. Or there is the three-year diploma course. In some places you can still train at a hospital, but basically all the training is done in colleges, going out to hospitals to gain your clinical skills. Apart from the academic and clinical skills required, there is far more to being a physiotherapist. 'You need the ability to be able to get on with people, talk to them and understand,' explains Ann Longden. 'You've got to be a counsellor, as well as being capable of doing the physical aspects. You must have good theoretical knowledge, so you know what you are doing practically.'

Working for the NHS, once qualified, you will probably be paid about the same as a college lecturer. Hours are normally day-time, with some weekend work, for which you will get paid extra. There is also emergency work, which you could involve you being on call at nights or over the weekend, so you can't stray too far.

Some clinical interest groups are for Riding for the Disabled, which is an opening for those interested in working with disabled people, using riding as a form of therapy.

Animal Physiotherapy

There is no formal training for animal physiotherapy; it is usually developed by physiotherapists who have an interest in animals, particularly dogs and horses. Despite the lack of formal training there are different clinical interest groups within the world of physiotherapy, a few of which are specifically for animals, as Ann explains:

> 'The Association of Chartered Physiotherapists in Animal Therapy is the clinical interest group concerned with treating animals. I only do animals because friends will phone me up, or somebody will say, "I've got a problem with a horse, Ann. Can you come and have a look at it?" With regard to the law, I wouldn't treat even a close friend's dog or horse without first getting in touch with their vet and having a good talk with him about it. I think the point with alternative therapy is to build up a good relationship with your local vets.
>
> 'I have notified my local vets that I am here, and I'm available and all this sort of thing. It's up to them, but they don't refer. It tends to be because I know people in the horse and dog world, and they suggest to their vet that they would like to try me. People will say, "Give Ann a ring; see what she thinks."'

Training

As with McTimoney Chiropractic, to be an animal physiotherapist, you must first train and qualify as a chartered physiotherapist in the human field. Entry requirements are similar to those for veterinary surgeons – a minimum of five GCSEs and two A levels. GCSE subjects should included passes in English, and at least two science subjects; the A levels should include a biological science. Alternatively, a BTEC National Diploma in Science (Level III), or a science Higher National Diploma may be considered. Most students train at universities; however, you can also train at one of several specialist schools of physiotherapy, usually attached to hospitals.

Once qualified as a chartered therapist, you will have the suffix MCSP (Member of Chartered Society of Physiotherapists). In order to qualify as an animal physiotherapist, you have to have a minimum of two years postgraduate experience working with humans before you can become a pupil with a veterinary practice or animal physiotherapist.

You remain a pupil until two veterinary surgeons are prepared to certify that you have successfully transferred your skills from humans to animals. This part of the training is then replaced by a validated course in animal therapy. It can be seven years or more before you can specialise in treating horses, so a lot of hard work and dedication, as well as academic skills, are needed to succeed.

Equine Dentist

In Britain, the demand for equine dentists is growing rapidly. Like many specialist branches of horse care, most veterinary surgeons do not have enough knowledge and experience to be the best person for the job. James Stokes has been a practising horse dentist for seven years.

> 'There is no formal training or qualifications for horse dentists in this country. Instead, I served an apprenticeship with a renowned equine dentist in Yorkshire. I stayed with him for over two years, learning all about the horse's mouth, the types of teeth and all the problems that can occur. I also ride myself, which helps. People often consult me when they have bitting or steering problems, and often I'll know the problem before I've looked into the horse's mouth.'

Most horse dentists will recommend six-monthly examinations for horses between three and six years old, because that is the most beneficial time. Horses' teeth cannot be straightened, but they can be rasped in ways that will prevent them becoming a problem.

In horses over seven years, it is unusual to find tooth decay unless a tooth has split, because the teeth have hardened considerably. Rasping older horses' teeth requires a lot of brute strength, and as with adult

humans, the work also involves removing build-ups of excess tartar.
James explains:

> 'A horse's head is the most sensitive area. You need to be quiet and slow when you're handling it, so as not to alarm or upset the horse. By law, I cannot use drugs to sedate the horses, so during treatment I use a "gag", which is a metal device that fits comfortably into the horse's mouth to prevent him closing it. This saves using the old method of holding the tongue out, which upsets the animal and can result in injury to both horse and dentist! I get a lot of referrals from vets, which is gratifying, considering I'm doing them out of a fee.'

James covers a wide area and his running costs are high; the fee he charges per animal needs to reflect these overheads. Your own success will depend upon the area you cover and the density of the horse population within it. If you wish to train as an equine dentist, you must either study in the USA, or find an established horse dentist who will take you on as an apprentice. It is a very rewarding and worthwhile career, but because it is hard physical work, many equine dentists seek alternative work when they become 'middle-aged'.

Finally, it goes without saying that working with horses in the field of medicine is one of the most rewarding jobs you could have in the industry, but you need to be the right sort of person to succeed – practical, with a brain.

Note: The law concerning the treatment of animals in the United Kingdom enables an owner to treat his own animals as long as he does not enter their bodily cavities, and someone may treat his employer's animals, with the same restriction, as long as they are in direct employment. Otherwise, only qualified veterinary surgeons may treat animals. No-one is allowed to treat an animal without a vet's permission, yet there are an awful lot of people doing just that, whether they be 'pretend' medical people, qualified by a society or whatever. Many don't realise, or wish to know, that it is against the law.

Chapter 6

Job Hunting and Employment

JOB HUNTING

Where To Look

Horse and Hound is the most popular choice when looking for work in the horse industry. It advertises jobs for grooms, instructors and stable managers, horse-associated positions, such as secretarial or sales work and overseas vacancies. Local papers and job centres are also a good source of vacancies, particularly if you want to stay close to home.

Employment agencies usually advertise in the equestrian press and it is worth registering with them to find work. Registration should be free; agencies are prohibited by law from charging fees to workers for finding or seeking to find them a job. You must send a full CV (to include qualifications, working history and personal details) and a description of the type of work you are interested in. The agency will send your details to prospective employers and supply you with details of immediate vacancies. Personal contacts in the industry are useful, and if you have earned a reputation for being a professional groom, you may find better opportunities are available 'on the grapevine'. A lot of jobs, particularly the more prestigious ones, are found by word of mouth. Reputation and good references go a long way in this industry.

Studying Job Adverts

Choosing which job to apply for is not just a simple matter of deciding which one provides the most pay and perks. By attempting to sort out the genuine from the exploitive, you can eliminate a great deal of unhappiness and wasted time in your career. How an advert is worded can be a good clue as to what the employer isn't telling you!

> GIRL FRIDAY required to look after two ponies and one horse. Qualifications not essential, experience is. Must weigh below nine stone and be good with children. £50 per week, live as family. Willingness to 'muck in' essential.

'Girl Friday' means that you will be doing anything and everything. Unless you love children and want to work with them, avoid all adverts that mention 'children's pony' or 'some babysitting required'. While babysitting is a good way of earning extra money, some employers expect you to babysit for free because you are on or near their premises. Willingness to 'muck in' can mean anything, from housework, dog walking, gardening to farm work.

No one can expect a high turn-out of horses and good standards of stable management if you have to do the hoovering, weed the garden and milk the cow! You want to work with horses, remember! If you don't mind doing extra duties, fair enough, you may enjoy being 'part of the family', but make sure your wages reflect the additional responsibility. Remember also that this type of job will do little to further your career as a professional groom and rider.

> INSTRUCTOR REQUIRED, BHSPI or equivalent. To assist BHSI and two trek leaders with busy riding school. Duties involve mainly teaching and sharing routine stable tasks. Good wage with full board for right applicant.

This job needs someone who is not only qualified to teach but also prefers teaching to riding. 'Duties involve mainly teaching' means you won't be riding much, if at all, so you've really got to love teaching and not mind that you won't have much opportunity to improve your own riding. You could ask if tuition from the BHSI on the yard could be part of your contract, but in a busy riding school the staff and trainee lessons always come second to the paying public.

> EVENT GROOM required. Excellent pay and accommodation. High standards of turn-out and stable management needed. Effective riding and understanding of fitness programmes required. Excellent opportunities for the right applicant. Present groom recommends.

Understandably, the more that is expected of you by way of skills and experience, the more you should expect to be paid. Such jobs as this are usually well paid, which is why the employer goes to great lengths to emphasise the high standards required and discourage anyone who may not be capable. It is up to you to prove that you are capable. 'Excellent opportunities' could mean the chance to compete, or at least get professional tuition. 'Present groom recommends' is a popular statement, in real terms it means, 'we will not exploit you'!

Applying for a Job

When an advert states 'apply in writing', do so, enclosing a neatly written, concise letter of application, a CV and copies of any references you have. First impressions last, make sure your letter and CV do you full justice. These guidelines apply to all jobs you apply for within the industry.

If you are not sure how to compose a letter of application and CV then use the following as a guide.

8 Green Drive
NEWTOWN
Newshire
NH22 6AB
Tel 0123 45678

21 January 1996

Dear Mr Brown

I would like to apply for the position of stable girl as advertised in the 'Horse Journal', dated week beginning 20 January 1996.

I have ridden since I was twelve, had two weeks' work experience with show jumpers and have worked with hunters and point-to-point horses for three years. I would like the job of stable girl because I am keen to pursue a career in racing. I am 20 years old, 5ft 7" and weigh nine stone. I am a non smoker and holder of a clean, current driving licence.

I enclose my CV and references for your perusal.

Yours sincerely

Lee MacKenzie

Lee MacKenzie
enc

Your address should be at the top of the letter to one side, your phone number is optional, but useful in speeding up a reply. If there is no name to address the letter to, 'Dear Sir or Madam' will suffice.

Mention the position you are applying for and the name and date of the publication it was advertised in. This is important in establishing for the employer exactly what position you are after. He or she may have several job vacancies advertised, and not all in the same publication.

Keep your riding and career history brief, do not repeat what is already on your CV. Mentioning your height and weight is important when applying for jobs with horses, particularly if you will be riding ponies, young animals or racehorses. Mention that you are a non-smoker as this is an advantage with most jobs. Smoking is a fire hazard around horses, so most employers will see smokers as a fire risk, however good their qualifications are. Stating that you are the holder of a clean, current driving licence increases your worth considerably. The more professional your letter looks, the better. What you write on is as important as the content of your letter. Good quality, unlined writing paper should be used and write with a black or blue pen only. Consider typing or word-processing your letter.

If your letter and CV are typed, consistency of punctuation, style and layout are important if you want to impress. Watch your spelling; nothing looks worse than bad spelling on a job application. It may be oversight on your part rather than lack of spelling skills, but both are avoidable if you check carefully or get someone to check for you. Remember, this is the first impression an employer has of you. A letter and CV that are professionally drafted will immediately create the right impression.

If you are just out of school and applying for a training position, then you may feel you do not have much information to justify a CV. Think carefully about everything you achieved at school. Were you in a sports team of some sorts, were you captain? Did you initiate any fund-raising events or school activities? Have you received any special awards or recognition for your talents, whether it be sport, academic or social? Were you involved in any school-related extra-curricular activities such as editor or reporter on the school magazine, drama class or representative for your school in a sports team or debating society? Success in any sphere will indicate ability to achieve in your career. Extra-curricular activities have potential to impress a prospective employer or training establishment, as well as improving your knowledge, communication skills and self-confidence.

CURRICULUM VITAE

Lee MacKenzie
8 Green Drive, Newtown, Newshire, NH22 6AB
Telephone 0123 45678

Date of Birth: 6 December 1975 Marital Status: Single

Schools Attended
St Helen's Primary School and Newtown High School, Newtown

Qualifications
Five GCSEs: English (A), Biology (A),History (B), Maths (C), Physical Education (C)

Additional Qualifications
Pony Club Test Standards D-B, ABRS Stable Helpers Certificate, Duke of Edinburgh Bronze and Silver Awards

History of Employment
While At School: Two weeks' work experience with show jumper Ted Robson. Duties involved mucking out, yard maintenance, grooming, tack cleaning and exercising horses.
September 1991 to present day: Three years working for Ketterly Hunt Master. Work involved general stable duties, grooming, exercising hunters and point-to-pointers. Preparing and travelling with horses.

Additional Experience/Sports and Hobbies
Captain of school swimming team, Reporter on School Newspaper. Swimming, squash and photography

If the advertisement has only a telephone number, then before you ring up, have a pen and paper ready to take notes of any details given not mentioned in the advert. Ask everything you need to know before committing yourself to attend an interview. Remember to get the directions if you are asked to come for an interview. It's easy to forget the obvious if you are nervous or excited about applying for a job, and you will feel foolish having to ring up again for further information.

Try to sound articulate, confident and cheerful when you speak, even if it is not to the person who will be employing you. Smile when you speak – it puts a smile in your voice! If the employer is not immediately available, leave your name and number and ask for the name and address of your employer. You then have the opportunity to send a formal letter of application and a CV which will be appreciated, and give you the edge over applicants who only phone. If you are offered the job over the phone, don't accept. You should be suspicious if an employer insists you start right away, without personal introduction or interview.

The Interview

Many employers are just as nervous and unprofessional about interviewing as people are about attending job interviews. There's a definite skill in being a successful interviewee. The main purpose of the interview is for you to 'sell yourself' to an employer and for the employer to 'sell a job' to you!

Dress

You will usually be required to ride during an interview for a job that involves handling horses, so that your riding abilities can be assessed. It's important to be physically and mentally comfortable with what you are wearing. You can't give of your best if you are worried that the jacket you borrowed looks unsuitable or too short! You will be under scrutiny for your skills as a rider, and if you are wearing new boots that are uncomfortable or a hat that is too big, then your riding will be affected.

You will usually be asked to come dressed to ride, but if you are travelling a long way, find out if there will be somewhere you can freshen-up and change for the interview. If you are not asked to ride or if you prefer, turn up in a smart outfit or suit and change later. This gives you the chance to show that you are professional not only in your riding, but also in your general outlook. As long as you are clean and sensibly dressed, it is not necessary to go out and buy new clothes which might be stiff or itchy and make you fidget.

For women, some make-up is flattering and can boost your confidence, but don't overdo it. Heavy make-up in broad daylight looks awful, and once you start riding you'll sweat, your make-up will run and you'll look and feel terrible. If you're hopeless at applying make-up, stick to the 'fresh faced' look! Perfume and aftershave are often sprayed on in haste, and in excess! Be warned, some scents can be disastrous when you are trying to prove you can handle a stallion or colt.

Travel Arrangements

Getting to the job interview on time should be your priority. If you are travelling by public transport, choose a departure time that allows for delays, long queues and rush-hour traffic. If you are travelling by car, either driving yourself or getting a lift, make allowances for traffic delays and petrol stops. If a breakdown or other unforeseen disaster should make you late, try if possible, to ring up and explain your predicament; when you get to the interview apologise profusely – this should clear the tension and get you off to a good start.

How you are interviewed will reflect the professionalism and fairness of your prospective employer. Try to relax. Appear happy and confident throughout your interview and in your dealings with other members of staff. Don't be condescending to junior members of staff or arrogant about your achievements. If you are asked a question and you don't know the answer, be honest and admit it; don't waffle. Creating a good impression means combining capability with modesty.

Have a pen and paper to take notes. Don't be embarrassed by this, it will show an employer that you are serious about your career. Most interviews begin with introductions, formal or informal, and are a useful guideline as to how the rest of the interview will be conducted. The employer should then explain the exact position offered, the environment you will be working in and the staff you will be working with.

You will then be asked questions relating to the information on your CV – for example, what your reasons are for wanting the job and what qualities you feel you can bring to the job. A good employer will also ask you what you want from the job and possibly what your long-term career ambitions are. If they don't ask, it is because they don't care.

Then it is your turn to ask questions. If an interviewer doesn't offer you the opportunity, take the initiative and ask anyway. Use this time to clarify all the points covered and ask about anything that has not been mentioned. Don't be frightened to ask if there are any hidden catches, such as having to muck out on your day off (not unusual!) or if wages mentioned are what you will receive in your hand. A wage may sound good until you find out you have to pay rent plus buy your own food and share the accommodation with five other grooms!

Sharing accommodation can be fun and it alleviates homesickness, provided that you all get on well and everyone is clear as to their responsibilities. There is nothing worse than having to live with someone who is untidy, self-centred or dirty in habits. Ask to meet the people you will be working and living with before making any commitment.

Insist on seeing the accommodation provided and ask where you will be sleeping. Some accommodation with horse jobs is excellent; good plumbing, heating, privacy and cleanliness are provided. You will often come in cold, wet and hungry when you have been working with horses and it doesn't help morale to have a poorly heated house, ineffective plumbing and dirty cooking facilities.

When you ride for the interview, being calm and confident will help you to stay in control. If you are asked to do something and you didn't hear correctly, ask for the instruction to be repeated, otherwise you will look incompetent if you perform the task incorrectly. Your riding will be assessed according to the standard required. The previous experience you claim to have had will be taken into consideration. When starting out with horses, an employer won't expect you to ride perfectly if you have limited experience. Your riding can only get better; what is more important is your enthusiasm and willingness to learn.

If you apply for a job and state that you are a competent rider, then that is what an employer will expect, and you must be prepared to show that you are. In professional yards you will be expected to ride all sorts of horses. Not all will be schoolmasters – often you are employed to ride youngsters and horses in need of re-training and discipline. Horses that are being fittened-up, for whatever purpose, can be fresh and play up sometimes, even if they are basically well behaved, so you must show some confidence and ability.

After riding, you may be asked to perform some stable management duties. Don't be nervous, and always remember the safety aspect of what you are doing. Afterwards, you may be asked questions on such things as minor ailments. The more you are pushed and tested in an interview, the more highly you may think of the job. Look at it from the employer's point of view. If they are offering good wages and perks, accommodation, opportunities to compete or travel, then they are entitled to the best grooms. You have to persuade them that you are worthy of the position and that you are willing and able to earn your wage. An honest day's work for an honest day's pay is the ideal. Here is a checklist of questions that should be answered by your employer. Don't be embarrassed to ask if there are any topics they do not discuss with you:

- *A detailed job description:* Remember to ask if there will be any extra work expected of you that is not related to horses.
- *Wages:* What will be your weekly gross pay, estimated net pay after

tax deductions and take-home pay after further deductions for rent, food, horse's keep etc.? How often will the wages be paid – weekly or monthly – and in what form, cash or cheque?

- *Annual holiday entitlement:* Are you entitled to holiday pay, if so, how much? Are there any restrictions on when you can take your holidays? At this point you should inform your employer of any holidays that you have already arranged and paid for. This will ensure you get the time off.
- *Days off:* How often? At least one day a week should be expected. Some employers arrange a weekend off once a month or a long weekend every two or three months. If you are the only groom working for this employer, you often find that days off can become fewer and farther between. This is exploitation and you should not tolerate it. A decent employer will make adequate arrangements to cover for you on your days off. Don't allow yourself to be pressured into working without a break; it is exactly this situation that causes physical exhaustion and leads to disillusionment.
- *Rules of conduct:* There have to be rules of conduct in any working environment to ensure a pleasant working atmosphere for the benefit of everyone, as well as the health and safety of all concerned, animals included. If you are not happy with any of the rules laid down, say so now. There should always be room for negotiation in the working life of grooms. Once you have accepted a job, it is harder to get things changed; an employer can take acceptance of the job as an agreement to abide by the rules and conditions.

Employment

Once you have succeeded in finding a job, bear in mind that your interests are protected by laws, so it is worth remembering the following before you accept a job, and once you have started.

Written Contracts of Employment

By law, it is necessary for a contract of employment to exist as soon as an employee proves their acceptance of an employer's terms. Both employer and employee are bound by the terms offered and agreed. The contract must be confirmed in writing within thirteen weeks of an employee starting work. The employer must give the employee a written statement containing certain important terms of employment, with an additional note, usually referring to disciplinary and grievance procedures. A written contract of employment between employer and employee, however, will normally refer to all the terms and conditions that have been agreed. Speaking personally, apart from my work in racing stables and during my BHS training, I was never offered a contract. A lot of dissatisfaction could be avoided if both parties have a written statement of terms to abide by; it safeguards both employer and employee rights. However, you are not entitled to a written statement if you are:

- Not an employee (i.e. you are an independent contractor or you work freelance).
- Working less than sixteen hours per week, unless you have been employed continuously by your employer for at least eight hours a week for at least five years.
- Engaged in work wholly or mainly outside the UK, unless you ordinarily work in the UK and the work outside the UK is for the same employer.

The written statement must include:

- The names of the employer and employee.
- The date when the employment began.
- The rate of pay, including overtime pay (many employers offer time off 'in lieu' rather than money for overtime worked).
- Terms and conditions of hours of work.
- Terms and conditions relating to holiday entitlement, including public holidays and holiday pay, sick pay and pension schemes.
- Length of notice of termination which you are obliged to give and entitled to receive, or, if the contract is temporary, the date when it expires. Length of notice is usually weekly or monthly, unless otherwise agreed.
- Title of the job which you are employed to do.

A detailed job description of the duties you are expected to perform stops you being conned into doing extra work, such as gardening, housework and babysitting (all common demands of unscrupulous employers). Unless you agree to additional duties, it is unfair of an employer to request you do extra work on top of your duties as a groom. However, if horses are out at grass for their holiday and you are still being paid, you may find yourself spring cleaning the yard, re-painting jumps and washing rugs. This is part of the routine of stable maintenance and is to be expected.

Finally, before you start training or working with horses, get yourself insured; at the very least, you need to be covered for accidents, including temporary and permanent disability, such as loss of use of limbs, and if you have dependants, life insurance is also a must. Working directly with horses can be risky – although serious accidents with horses are rare, don't kid yourself that it will never happen to you.

Chapter 7

Self-Employment

Self-employment, either working freelance or starting your own business, is the ultimate ambition for many of us. As we move towards the twenty-first century, patterns of work are changing. The old idea of working for one employer for forty hours a week, for forty years is dying. As is the notion that when a woman marries, she will give up work to look after her husband and family. The eighties, with its dramatic drop in the number of school leavers and the consequent reduction in the male workforce, has brought 'career women' to the forefront. Women want to make a career out of horses, not just a stop-gap before marriage. These changes have also affected the equestrian industry. Racing, in particular, now employs far more women than it did in the sixties and seventies.

In general, people are changing not only their jobs, but also their entire careers and gearing their careers towards setting up their own business or offering their services freelance. Perhaps you have always been interested in horses and are considering giving up work in a non-related industry (or have been made redundant) and you want to combine your training and experience with your interest in horses to set up your own equestrian enterprise.

Realising that you will never get rich looking after someone else's horses, the romantic notion of taking charge of your own future, of creating your own work and having the freedom to choose what work you do, is a very attractive proposition. However, if you like the security of a regular salary, perhaps you will not be as suited to self-employment as you may think.

Finding the capital to start up and run a business isn't easy, but you could compromise and have a part-time job which provides a regular income whilst you develop your business in the other half of your time.

Self-employment is not all success and security. There are risks; cash-flow can be a tremendous problem – creditors, such as feed merchants and vets, are not going to wait to be paid until your customers have paid you, so you need to make sure that you have enough capital to keep you going. Most new businesses find the first two years is a time of very hard work, long hours, little pay and no holidays. Although you haven't a boss looking over your shoulder, the standards and goals that you set for yourself will be even more demanding.

TYPES OF SELF-EMPLOYMENT

Most people view self-employment as working on your own as a sole trader; however, franchising and partnerships are also types of self-employment.

Sole Trader: This term usually means a self-employed person working on their own, and is the most common option for those taking up self-employment. The term is also used when the self-employed person employs others. Becoming a sole trader is the simplest way to start your own business. There are few formalities to go through, although you will need to notify the Inland Revenue and the Department of Social Security. If working from home, you may need planning permission, depending on the type of business you intend to start.

As a sole trader, you will have the advantage of being in total control of the business and reap all the glory and the profits. On the other hand you get all the problems as well. Although you can seek professional advice, you are very much on your own. It can be lonely, and you will need a lot of self-discipline to achieve your aims. The legal disadvantage of being a sole trader is that you do not have limited liability – if you go bankrupt your creditors are entitled to seize not just your business assets but also your personal possessions.

Partnerships: A partnership is a business formed by between two and twenty people, which is not registered as a co-operative or a company. It can be set up without any written or verbal agreement between the partners although, sensibly, most partnerships do start with a written agreement. Usually partners buy their way into a firm, be it new or existing. They do not always contribute the same amount of money – for example, one partner may own a third of the business, one may own two thirds. Profits are shared according to the size of your shareholding.

Partnerships do not usually have limited liability, which means that if your firm goes into liquidation, the partners are personally liable for its debts. This liability is not divided in relation to the size of the shareholding, each partner is equally liable – so be careful who you go into partnership with. Business partnerships are like marriage: they may last a life-time, or erupt into a messy divorce; and if your partner runs off, you will be left with the responsibilities, no matter what agreements you have put in writing.

If you decide to form a partnership, be it with family, friends or business associates, get a formal deed of partnership drawn up by a solicitor, in which you define your roles, voting rights, sharing of the profits etc.

The best advantage of being a partnership is that you are not alone – you are part of a team sharing strengths, skills and worries, not to mention the profits and costs. You have others to plan with, and invariably a team of people can create far more ideas and generate more output than one person alone.

Franchising: The horse industry offers very few opportunities to buy an existing franchise unless you are considering an associated trade. However, there is nothing to stop you from starting up your own franchise, whether it be directly involved with horses or in an associated trade, such as merchandising or saddlery. Franchising is one way of reducing the risks of self-employment without losing all the rewards as, although you will be your own boss, you are not alone because you have the support of the franchiser.

If you come up with the right idea and marketing tactics, by setting up your own franchise you will not only reap the profits from your own outlet but also earn a considerable amount of money selling your franchise to others who wish to establish their own shop or business in a different area.

The British Franchise Association (BFA) defines franchising as, 'The method by which the owner of a business (franchiser) contractually agrees to allow another independent person or company (franchisee) to market its products or service within a specified geographical area. In return, the franchisee pays an initial fee for the rights to the area and a royalty on sales giving the franchiser a percentage benefit on sales.'

When choosing a franchise aimed at the horse industry, think very carefully about the market you're going for; what is successful in one area may not be in another, for several reasons. Franchising still requires a lot of local market research on your part. Think carefully about location, and do speak to other franchisees if possible. When it comes to choosing a suitable franchise, bear in mind that the franchiser is trying to sell something, so read any information sent to you very carefully – especially the small print.

Sources of Help

Most people need some support in their work – someone to talk over ideas and problems with. You may be relying on family to assist and support you, but their judgement can be weakened by consideration for your feelings and for their own welfare. There are several independent organisations which offer advice and assistance such as the Prince's Youth Business Trust (PYBT) and the Rural Development Commission (RDC). In addition to all the normal grants and types of help available to the self-employed, there are also extra forms of help for the disabled; for example, grants are available to convert premises to make them suitable for someone with a disability. For more information contact the Disablement Resettlement Officer (DRO) at your local job centre, or the Disabled Living Foundation in London.

Both practical and business skills are needed in self-employment. Luckily there is a great deal of professional advice, training, support and financial help in the shape of grants and loans, available for both currently and potentially self-employed people. Finding your way through the maze of grants, loans and schemes can be very confusing as, for example, some grants are only available to people of certain ages or who wish to work in specific areas of the country. The organisations which offer these types of help are constantly changing and developing new ways of assisting the self-employed. Because of this, the best place to start finding out about becoming self-employed is at your local Enterprise Agency, who are likely to be absolutely up-to-date with all the sources of available help and who are particularly able to give initial assistance to those wishing to become self-employed.

Enterprise Agencies (EAs) is a collective term for organisations whose main aim is to offer a free service of counselling, support and advice to people wanting to set up in self-employment and to small firms wishing to expand. They consist of a partnership between public and private sector organisations and are located throughout the country operating under a variety of names. Your local authority will know where you can get in touch with the Enterprise Agency in your area.

These agencies offer advice and help on anything to do with starting self-employment, such as sources of grants, other sources of help, financial and legal advice and how to find suitable premises. They also offer a great deal of support, such as helping you prepare a business plan.

Local authorities vary enormously in the amount of financial help they can offer. At one end of the scale there are authorities which offer nothing whatsoever, and at the other end, there are authorities offering a great deal including grants for equipment, for new buildings or to convert unused space. In some cases, there may be assistance with rents or rates. Most authorities will be able to offer some help and advice to newcomers to self-employment. The switchboard of your local town/county/shire hall will be able to put you in touch with the appropriate department.

Many colleges of further education and adult education centres funded by local authorities offer courses in setting up your own business. Also, some authorities have initiatives to help the self-employed.

The Business Start-Up Programme is a Government scheme funded by the Employment Department and run by independent agencies. Before this scheme was introduced, an unemployed person starting self-employment would lose their benefit from the moment they started work, even though it could be months or even years before they were able to earn enough money to live on. The Business Start-Up Scheme means that as an unemployed person starting self-employment, you are entitled to receive a weekly allowance on top of your benefits.

Many people in the horse industry have started their businesses on this scheme, including instructors, horse dealers, farriers, saddlers, rug makers and employment agents. As well as the financial benefits, it also offers help and advice in all aspects of starting up a business. To find out whether you are eligible and what the allowances are, contact your job centre or employment office.

The Prince's Youth Business Trust (PYBT) is a charity which helps young people up to the age of thirty to set up or develop their own businesses, but its underlying aim is greater than that. As its mission statement puts it, 'It helps young people, who would not otherwise have the opportunity, to develop their self-confidence, achieve economic independence, fulfil their ambitions and contribute to the community through the medium of self-employment.'

Applicants must have a viable business idea and the enthusiasm and determination to succeed. You must also have tried but failed to raise all the necessary finance – the Trust is a source of 'last resort' funding. As well as funding, the Trust also offers crucial help and advice for your business. Everyone who receives money from the Trust is allocated a business advisor who will spend a few hours each month to keep an eye on how your business is going and offer you advice. Valuable marketing opportunities are also available. The Trust not only stages an annual trade show of its own, but it also arranges space in other exhibitions enabling you to display your wares to large and appropriate audiences.

The Rural Development Commission's stated aim is, 'To assist in the regeneration of the rural areas of England by stimulating the success of small businesses which contribute to local prosperity and help to improve the quality of life in the countryside'. In order to do this, they offer a wide range of help from advising on how to start your own business, to regular visits to offer advice and support once you are established. They will help you to get a loan from a bank, and in some cases, may have loans or grants to offer you themselves. They also offer advice and training courses in both business management and the practical skills needed for a rural business.

The Highlands and Islands Development Board and the Scottish Development Agency in Scotland, and the Development Board for Rural Wales offer similar services.

Tourist Boards publish a number of leaflets which can be of use to those setting up in self-employment in the tourist industry, and those already in business. They will give advice and guidance and can offer grants to help with building costs, for example, to make facilities accessible for disabled riders at a riding centre. If your proposed business involves people coming to the area to enjoy it, then the Tourist Boards may be able to help you.

THE BUSINESS

You have three choices when going into business: you can buy into an existing business as a partner; you can buy a business outright; or you can start a new business from scratch. This is what most people aim to do, and it is the one which needs the most careful thought.

Business Planning: Any business needs careful thought and proper planning before you can take your proposals to banks, trusts or other suppliers of funds. First, you must decide what you want to do. Opportunities within the horse world for setting up a business include such diversities as freelance instructor, livery schools, horse trainer, riding holiday centres, stud farms, horse retail, farriery, equine veterinary clinics, alternative therapist, equine marketing consultant – the list is endless! It is up to you to decide which type of business will best suit your skills, family commitments and financial resources.

Many equestrian businesses are run to standard ideals, for example, 'I have my BHSI, I have the necessary premises and financial backing to set up a riding school – so that is what I'll do.' It's not enough to just decide that you are going to run a riding school then let the business take its own course. You must get down on paper a formal business plan – setting down what you are doing, why you are doing it and how you could do it better. In practice, most equestrian establishments should devote more time to thinking about the future of their business – it is the added discipline and focus of putting these plans down on paper and critically analysing each alternative strategy that is missing.

For some, just running a horse-orientated business is enough – but if you refuse to look at it in anything but a romantic light, you will not be doing full justice to your skills and potential. Making a profit and surviving is one thing, but you should also think about why you are where you are and how best to exploit the advantages you have. For example, one riding school may offer polo lessons, attracting customers – particularly men – who may not have been interested in riding before, but who will initially need several ordinary lessons to learn to ride before taking up the sport. This will help to achieve your objective of increasing turnover, then you can invest in more horses, or build leisure facilities such as a restaurant, bar or clubhouse. You may have to start small, but by careful planning you can continually expand your business.

Budgeting: By providing a framework for detailing all your short-term plans in financial terms, you can monitor your detailed performance, taking any necessary action. For example, the riding school can keep a separate budget of polo lessons and ordinary lessons which stem from them, so that it can see the effects of offering polo lessons on the rest of the business.

Three elements – objectives, plans and budgeting – are the basis of business planning. The level of detail may vary: the riding school proprietor will have less requirement for regular detailed reports than say, a retail company that sells equestrian sportswear. However, a regular analysis of turnover and profit by the sale of horses, rental of school and riding lessons will tell him where his profits are coming from and perhaps, where his business is going to.

Many books have been written on business planning and corporate strategy, all of which can be applied to equestrian businesses. Your local library usually has a good selection of these books for your perusal and will be of invaluable help in your research. Also, through horse book shops you can buy books specifically about managing a horse business.

Marketing

Marketing is an area most equestrian businesses neglect; those that don't are highly successful and profitable, and in return receive a lot of publicity within the equestrian press, which in itself is a good marketing strategy – success breeds success. 'You can't make money out of horses,' snorted one riding school proprietor to me. I would say that she, and all the other equestrian proprietors who make that statement are not marketing their products or services nearly as effectively as they could be, and that these people are not running a business, but scratching a living from their love of horses.

Every business idea requires careful research. Whether it is a service or product – or both – you must find out who your customer will be, what he wants (not necessarily what you have in mind to offer), at what price (be realistic about this and don't under-sell your services or products just to get on the market – many new business make this mistake and fail as a result), at what time (equestrian businesses such as studs or riding centres tend to be busier in summer than in winter), and finally where – the right location can mean death or glory for a new business.

Who is your customer? This will depend upon the service or product you have to offer. However, you should ask the customer what he wants, then tailor-make your business to suit that purpose. You must establish at the outset exactly who your customer will be and keep a mental picture of that customer in your mind when considering the other criteria of your business.

If you are selling exclusive hand-made riding boots, then your customer will usually be a professional sportsman ready to invest a good deal of money into a decent pair of boots, so don't underprice them because that in itself can discourage people from buying. If your boots are the best money can buy, then your prices should reflect that. When advertising in the equestrian press, choose periodicals aimed at the professional riders, such as *Horse and Hound* or *Eventing*. You can also offer a service whereby customers can take the opportunity to visit you personally for fittings.

Alternatively, if you are running a riding school, it is equally important to keep your customers, by keeping their interests and needs as a top priority. This is the philosophy of one of Britain's leading marketing consultants, Alan Newton, who found the riding schools in his area desperately lacking in customer awareness.

'I used to go horse riding,' explains Alan. 'I went to one place but didn't return. I didn't like the way they treated the horses. They seemed scruffy; no-one seemed to care about it. Actually, going out on the horse was alright; I really enjoyed it. It was the stables, they looked unkempt, and all the horses looked scruffy. I thought, "I don't want to support them to keep these horses in filth," but nobody ever asked my opinion. Nor did they ask, "Did I enjoy it?", or, "What I would like to see offered?"'

You may advertise as having the best qualified instructors, or best hacking country in the area, but people's opinions of instructors change when they see the state of the yard. Alan says:

> 'In the horse industry, there is a divided market. Like anywhere else, there is a proportion of businesses which are at the bottom end of the scale. It is true that some people will choose a riding school or a stallion because the price is low. It's a very small proportion, however, compared with other industries, because most of the people who go horse riding or keep horses care about the animals, and therefore there is a great need to emphasise the top end of the market, which is on quality. With regard to riding schools, it is not being catered for enough.
>
> 'The riding schools I've been to didn't inspire me to go back, although the actual riding was okay. For example, in one riding school I rode on the beach and among the dunes, and it was great fun – but it was chucking it down with rain. I had to come back, get off outside, soaking wet, and stand for ten minutes before somebody took my horse from me. I was wet, mucky and cold and I had to get back into my ordinary car (I don't have a Land Rover to mess about in). I had to sit in my car, getting it wet and dirty, and drive home in that state. I would have loved to have gone in for a shower, or at least had somewhere to dry myself off, then have a glass of beer or mug of coffee – like the old sports club syndrome. How about shower facilities, changing rooms, and after the ride a place to eat and drink? Nobody seemed to think about it because they were covered in muck all the time and used to working in wet weather.'

If you're thinking of running a riding school or trekking centre, why not incorporate a leisure centre, bar and restaurant, make it a whole day or evening event, particularly if you are in a tourist area and in competition with leisure and wildlife parks? Don't just offer an hour's ride, then once the client is back and off the horse, he's forgotten about. The larger studs and racing yards are customer-conscious – riding schools should be too.

Marketing should not used just at the outset of a business; it has to be an on-going thing, if your business is to keep up with its customers' needs and with the competition. You need a long-term marketing strategy; too many equestrian businesses are run on a hand-to-horse's-mouth basis, and the last thing you'll want to spend money on is marketing, even if you don't think you can afford to. Alan Newton again:

> 'Look at it creatively and ask yourself these questions: My business is in this area where there is a population of 300,000 people, do I know how many people ride or own horses? Do I know how many come to me every week? Do I know how much business I am actually missing?'
>
> 'The answer to all these questions is usually, no. You need somebody to help you. Okay, you may be getting £500 worth of business per week, but did you know, let's say, that there is £50,000 a week spent on horses in this region alone. Either you must be prepared to take time out from running your business to find out about your market, or you must employ someone to do it for you – preferably a marketing consultant with experience of the equestrian and tourism industry.
>
> 'You need a lot of psychology to work out why people do things. For example, someone may have a choice of half a dozen places to go to ride. Why do they choose one place above the other? Why aren't they choosing yours? Has anybody ever asked them – it's unlikely.'

These are exactly the sort of questions a marketing consultant will find the answers to. If you are a small company, you may only require a consultant to come out for one day a month to see how the business is prospering. He or she will take a good look at your cash-flow and show up the areas where you can save money, or where you should be investing more money. In the long term, a marketing consultant will increase your profits in two ways; first, by finding ways to cut back on costs, and second, by coming up with new ideas to increase and sustain customer interest.

Be honest with yourself, are you really capable of looking at your business objectively and taking the time to find out all the relevant facts and figures for market research – if not, pay someone else to. The money you spend on a good marketing consultant will pay dividends for you in the long run.

Location

The area in which you set up a business will depend on the nature of the business and on premises available. You need to be where your customers are: e.g. a riding school should be within a ten-mile radius of at least three urban areas. Private trainers can afford to have their premises a little further out – if your reputation is good enough people will not mind travelling a reasonable distance to your yard.

Holiday riding centres that do not need to depend on daily clients can also be located further from urban areas; rural landscapes without heavy traffic are a big incentive for riding holiday enthusiasts. However, you will need to arrange transport from towns to your centre if your clients are arriving by plane, coach or train.

Racing yards need to be near to several racecourses with a good motorway nearby for access to distant racecourses. Stud farms also need good motorway access if owners are to be encouraged to travel mares to your stallion – however good he is, he must be within a reasonable and easily accessible distance.

Study a population map of the UK. It reveals that the bulk of the human population is situated in the South and Midlands of England; in Scotland it is in the South, around Glasgow and Edinburgh. Unless you are offering 'get away from it all' riding holidays, you should aim to be as near to towns and cities of reasonable populations as possible, if you are running a training yard or riding school. Places like Devon and the North of Scotland are great for equestrian tourism, but will put you at a disadvantage if you are trying to bring on and sell competition horses; no-one will travel such distances and the local horse scene in such areas will not provide sufficient interest. Retail shops can be urban, but need to be easily found, preferably on a main through-road, with parking facilities provided or very close by. Those that have room for horses to be unloaded are an advantage when someone is investing in a saddle or other specialist fittings.

Finance

Coming up with the capital to start a business isn't easy. It's a standard joke that bank managers only lend money to people who can show that they don't need it – ironically, there is an element of truth in this. If you are going to ask a bank for a large loan, you will need to show you can put up some collateral, such as mortgaging your property. Smaller loans require an assurance that you can come up with the money for repayments on a monthly basis. Banks will want to look at your personal cost of living and income. In either case, you must present a business plan and cash-flow forecast with a realistic estimate of what your outgoings and sales are going to be. At many of the agencies mentioned, particularly the Business Start-Up Scheme, you can learn about planning aids, which include resource planning, profit and loss, break-even points, distribution profiles etc. *The Directory of Grants and Trusts, Kompass* and the *Sponsorship Directory* all provide the names and addresses of companies, associations and private individuals who are prepared to offer financial help to people in their particular industry or personal interest.

Once your business gets the go-ahead, you will need to keep an eye on finances using a book-keeping system that is simple to operate. In business, money does two things: 'comes in' and 'goes out'. A good book-keeping system should show you what money is available to the business, what money the business owes and what money is owed to the business. This information will enable you to make financial decisions. Keep your records up-to-date and analyse them regularly. This way, you can be sure that you are meeting the sales targets you have set and do not go into serious debt.

Planning aids are a vital aspect of any business. It is best to keep two diaries. A year planner for the office wall, so that dates for shows, vets and farrier's visits and other important events can be seen at a glance, and a desk diary of clients, sales and purchases to show monthly and annual trends of busy periods for a riding school, types of horses bought from a dealing yard and the busiest periods of sale for a saddlery and clothing shop. This information can be transferred to a diagram to show trends to staff and advisors, such as your bank manager or marketing consultant.

A distribution profile is a valuable asset to the freelance trainer or instructor. You can use a large Ordinance Survey map of your area or compile your own simple chart. It will show the travelling time and associated costs and thus you can calculate the overall cost of the service you are offering.

A profit and loss chart will show your break-even point, the level of sales required to cover costs. Anything in excess of this figure will start to produce a net profit.

Advertising

This is the bridge between you and your customer. If you get the advertising right, you'll attract the right customer. To do that, your advertising needs to be informative, appealing and on-going. Advertising, like all aspects of business, requires a budget; you should look at all the options carefully, and if you have researched your market properly, this will also reveal where and when you should be advertising and how best to attract customer attention. Depending on the size and nature of your business, there are several ways in which you can promote your product or service.

Periodicals, in particular those aimed at equestrian professionals and enthusiasts, are a popular form of advertising for nationally available products or services. Alternatively, local newspapers are always on the look-out for new stories, and a new business in the area is often the basis for an interesting feature, particularly if you are offering something unique or a new service to the community. Your business, whether it is offering a product or service, will be best served by issuing a press release to the local and equestrian press; you could also include local radio and television, which offers publicity over a broader spectrum.

If you have a business line put into your office by British Telecom then you are entitled to a free line entry in *Yellow Pages.* Be very careful how you categorise your business so that you are in the right place in the book when a potential customer is looking for your specialism.

For businesses aimed at the tourist sector, a *card* or *brochure* can be placed in local pubs, restaurants, libraries, hotels, guest houses, leisure centres and theme parks. Make the most of local tourist information publications and the tourist information offices in your area.

Special Promotions can be in the form of open days, fêtes, competitions and sponsored events on your premises. If you are launching a prouct that will be sold nationally, you may wish to hire the services of a specialist promotional company. Although expensive, these companies will ensure that your product or service gets every possible exposure.

Trade Stands at agricultural, local and major horse shows and events will pay dividends, although they are expensive to start up. Initially, you will need a show stand, including protection from rain, tables for displaying goods and seats for tired passers-by (a great attraction!). Costs will include travel expenses and the booking fee for your place at the show or event.

If your business is equestrian based, then entering for *events* and *classes* will be a shop window for the horses and ponies you are selling, or in the case of riding schools and trainers, standards of training of which you are capable.

Finally, do bear in mind that the key to success is customer satisfaction. The horse world is a small world, and any amount of advertising is a waste of money if your establishment gets a bad reputation for poor standards and lack of customer care. No matter how much you advertise, people will always go to your rival. Offer clients value for money, a sense of achievement and a pleasant experience if they are to return and recommend you to others.

Europe

Expanding your business to another European Union member state is far less complicated than you imagine. Your local Government-funded business centre will be able to supply the necessary information on selling into Europe, as well as all the channels of support you have used to set up in business initially, e.g.: The Prince's Trust or The Rural Development Commission. Equestrian trade fairs in other member states are advertised in the British equestrian press, so whether you are standing a stallion or selling saddles, you should not overlook the financial benefits of expanding into Europe.

You also have the right to establish yourself as a self-employed person in a European Union state, with exactly the same rights as a national of that state. You will, however, have to comply with the conditions placed on that country's nationals for the type of business concerned. You will also be allowed to live there. This right of residence carries with it the opportunity to buy a house and to bring your family to live with you. You do not need a work permit, but you and each member of your family must obtain a long-term residence permit once you are there.

Opportunities in the Horse Industry

There are a considerable number of opportunities available if you are considering self-employment, both directly with horses, and in horse-associated trades. The options available will of course depend upon your own skills, qualifications and financial resources.

Horse dealer Alexandria Smith has ridden since the age of two. Taught by her mother and the Pony Club, Alexandria also did a lot of competing for other people, particularly on ponies and horses that were too hot and gassy for them to handle. After leaving school, she trained for working in the media, both selling and designing adverts, but she soon got tired of the office regime: 'Media work was okay, but in that sort of job you're on a set wage, it's straight nine-to-five work and I'm just not the kind of person who wants to be stuck in an office.'

Alexandria gave up media work and went on to teach children at an equitation centre:

> 'It was there that I found two ponies; they were both emaciated and full of mange. The ponies were quite a handful when I got them and it took me a few days just to get near them. Now they've turned out absolutely brilliant. I broke one in last summer, then sold him in January to a really good home. His owners use him for the Prince Philip Cup Games. I sold the other to a lovely home who wanted him for their granddaughter. I made good money on both ponies and got the satisfaction of seeing them go to deserving homes, and that's how I got started in horse trading.'

She then answered an advertisement in the local paper for a 14.2hh pony:

> 'It was with a typical dealer. She ended up selling me two incredibly thin ponies which were nothing like what I wanted. I bought the two for £600. After feeding them up and bringing them on I sold one for £850 and, a week later, sold the other for £750. Then it just took off from there. Since then, I've had some really good animals, and some crazy ones!
>
> 'You learn by your mistakes in this trade. There's a lot of dishonesty, far worse than the car trade. I started buying a lot of ponies from one dealer and was mortified to find out some had been stolen, so I don't deal with her any more. A lot of dealers have no scruples and can be quite cruel. People like that give horse dealers a bad name.'

Alexandria charges a reasonable price for her animals – some dealers are very expensive and get away with it because of who they are. She buys a lot off the trade, but sells privately:

> 'The only ones I sell back to the trade are the crazy ones. Some horses you feel sorry for – they've been round and round the dealers yards and are so screwed up it's dangerous to do anything with them. Consequently, it's impossible to find them good homes. I also save quite a lot from the knacker men, whom I loathe; most of the horses

prove to be really nice tempered, easy rides. A lot have been knocked about quite a bit and are so frightened you can't get near them to begin with.

'You don't need much capital to start with. I bought the first two ponies with my dole money. My grandmother lent me a couple of thousand and I went on from there. My overheads are high. I rent a stable block nearby with fifteen acres of land for £160 per month, which I like to pay up well in advance. My biggest outgoing is the blacksmith, but I believe in taking very good care of their feet! I've saved a lot on vets' bills by learning to do a lot of the veterinary side myself, like administering injections. I also have an excellent vet whom I can ring up for advice and I collect the medicines I need, which saves me a fortune on call-out fees.

'I deal in tack as well. It's not cheap, but I buy a lot at markets and riding schools that are closing down. A lot of people who buy horses from me are just starting out and need the equipment as well, so I keep a selection in stock to offer them – which helps to boost profits.

'You can make money on horses, but you've got to be careful because you can lose it just as easily. I recently lost £900 on one animal, and that's a lot to make up! I enjoy the wheeling and dealing in the trade, but I get cross with people who value their horses sentimentally, not realistically. At the moment I am making some good money out of the horses, but this is my first year in the trade so most of it goes back into buying stock. I don't pay taxes or VAT at the moment because I'm only just starting up.'

'All the horses I sell are guaranteed; if people aren't happy with them, I'll buy them back. Building up my reputation is important to me. I think of the horses as much as the client and try to match them up with suitable owners. If someone is really suited to a horse but can't afford the asking price, I'll take a gamble and let them pay so much in cash then the rest by post-dated cheques. Equally, if someone comes to try out one of my horses and is a hopeless rider or just not suited to that horse, I'll refuse to sell it and suggest they take riding lessons instead. It might sound rude, but it's not fair on the buyer and certainly not fair on the horse. I get a lot of people ringing up to say their friends have bought horses from me and can I find one for them. It's pleasing to know that my standards are paying off.'

Her successful marketing strategy also takes careful consideration of seasonal trends.

> 'The sort of horses I'm looking for at the moment are around 14.2hh. Nice, quiet rides – they sell best. But these are hardest to find so at the moment I've got a lot of buyers on my books but not the right horses for them. In the winter, it will be the hunters that sell. I deal mainly in ponies for games and jumping. My height and weight is an advantage in that I can ride smaller ponies without damaging them. Ideally, they should be between age four to ten and between 12.2 and 14.2hh. I've also got the knack for riding the fizzier, hard to handle ones which aren't easy for some dealers whose methods tend to make those sort of ponies even worse! I'd like to deal in show jumpers also; I've had a few, but at the moment I'm not in a position to keep horses for too long and put the time into them that they need – I need quite a rapid turnover to keep going. They're also a bit high-priced on the current market.

Alexandria has built up a reputation for being honest with people: 'If an animal has a vice or defect I tell the truth and take a chance that they will still buy. Okay, it doesn't always work, but it does pay to be honest in the end. I couldn't be the ruthless, unscrupulous type.' For anyone wanting to deal in horses, she advises:

> 'Take it very slowly to begin with. Start off with a couple of ponies. It does help to be careful about what you buy. You could buy lots of ponies and most will turn out to be useless. Be careful who you buy from, and don't pay too much for anything to start with, however promising they look. It does help to work in a dealing yard and learn the ropes, which is what I did for a short time, but a lot of what I learned I didn't approve of. You have to set your own standards. People think I'm ruthless and hard-hearted buying and selling, but I do get upset when I sell them on. It's not something I'll ever get used to, but at the end of the day it is my livelihood and I have to be business-like about it.'

Trade is good in the horse industry, at the moment it's not really suffering under the recession because it's still very much a growing industry. New products or services attract a lot of attention and can provide exciting business prospects. Vanessa Cheffing, BHSII, runs the Downe Farm Dressage Training yard in North Devon:

'When I passed my BHSPI, I ran a riding school/trekking yard on Exmoor with my husband and we moved from there to here. I did run a riding school here for a year or two, but it wasn't really what I wanted to do, also the hacking out around here, particularly for novice clients, wasn't safe enough.

'Mostly, I've done the odd hunter livery and a bit of breaking and schooling. When we left milk production, we diversified and got a grant to have our large barn altered to stables. The dressage side has really picked up since. We have people come in with their own horses that we teach and sometimes they leave their horses here for two or three weeks' schooling. I don't keep horses here for other people to ride. It's not a riding school.'

As well as offering dressage training, the farm also provides stud facilities and to Vanessa's delight, its stallion, the Danish Warmblood, De Beer, is already proving an excellent investment.

'He's broken-in and has been competing successfully under saddle. We take him to quite a lot of competitions. He has had a second in the National Intermédiaire Championships, so we're delighted with him. As for my long-term ambitions for him, I suppose one would have to say the Olympics. That's a way off yet, but not out of reach.'

Downe Farm Dressage Training Yard and the De Beer Stud is a good example of a business which has been thoroughly researched and managed to meet the customer's needs – a recipe for success. It is impossible to find a business idea or product that is instantly successful, particularly with horses, as so much depends on reputation and standards, and both take time to assert. However, if you have the persistence, the self-discipline and a good marketing strategy (the most important element of all), you can succeed.

Towards 2000

The next decade will be a very exciting time for the British horse industry. The future success of the industry will not only continue to prosper, but will enhance its reputation as the country to train in whatever your career plan. For employment, the horse industry has never looked more attractive and the prospects it generates will continue to provide a great future for all of us.

Chapter 8

Training

In recent years, the systems of training within the horse industry have undergone dramatic and exciting changes for the better. The prospect of training and working with horses is now considerably enhanced by the Government's recognition that the industry plays an important role as a source of training and as a career option. The horse industry itself also recognises that it must provide a solid foundation of training courses and examinations if young people are to come into the industry, and stay to make a career.

The Joint National Horse Education and Training Council (JNHETC) was formed in 1987 and has two principle responsibilities:

- *Lead Body:* concerned with the development of levels of qualifications and systems of quality assurance to the standard laid down by the Government through the National Council for Vocational Qualifications (NCVQ) and, in Scotland, the Scottish Vocational and Education Council (SCOTVEC).
- *Industry Training Organisation (ITO):* concerned with training policy matters and the delivery mechanisms which will benefit the industry as a whole.

This means that the JNHETC is now responsible for all training and education in the horse industry. It has two main committees, the Executive Committee, concerned with policy and financial matters and the Technical Committee which, as the name implies deals with the development of qualifications and other technical issues in the training field. The Quality Assurance Group aims to ensure consistency in the implementation of qualifications across the whole sector. Much of its work to date has involved the development and establishment of the National Vocational Qualifications (NVQs) and the Scottish Vocational Qualifications (SVQs).

THE NVQ LEVELS

National Vocational Qualifications are based on standards developed by industry to make qualifications even more relevant to work and, hopefully, more valued by employers. The NVQ levels are not examinations and are awarded through continuous assessment at the workplace, not at an examination centre. They are not a replacement of the existing horse industry exams but are designed to complement them by providing comparable standards of competence across the sector.

The object of NVQs is to give the candidate credit for what he/she actually does in a job. Each work area is covered in detail, observed by an assessor, with progress charted in a Record of Achievement booklet when the necessary standard is reached. Each element and unit of competence counts towards the final certificate. Candidates can develop at their own pace and build on previous successes. With the NVQs, candidates will be able to prove that they have reached a nationally recognised level of competence. Because the NVQs now apply to every industry, should employees wish to give up working with horses and re-train for a career outside the horse industry, parts of the NVQ qualifications will be recognised by the new employer. The levels will, eventually, also be recognised within the European Union.

NVQs in Horse Care

In addition to the compulsory Care Units listed below, specialist options are available for these qualifications – namely, Basic Riding Skills, the Racing Industry, Working Horses on the Land, Driving Horses and Breeding Horses. There are two routes candidates can take with the NVQs. Level I is common to both, with mandatory (care) units common to each route at levels II and III. Optional units apply to the specialist field chosen. Additional units, which are not part of the qualification, are also available.

NVQ Horse Care Level I – Generally, this is for an assistant working under supervision. It indicates that the candidate is competent in the performance of work activities which are mainly routine and predictable.

It provides foundation for the future development of skills.

Mandatory Units
Assisting with routine care: Servicing facilities; Handling horses from the ground; Preparing horses for use under supervision; Liaising with callers and colleagues.

NVQ Horse Care Level II and Racehorse Care Level II – This level covers skills with more responsibility. It indicates that the successful candidate is competent in a broader and more demanding range of work activities. This level involves greater individual responsibility than Level I.

NVQ Horse Care Level II

(a) Mandatory Units
Providing routine care; Preparing horses for use; Determining health and condition; Working horses from the ground; Contribute to providing grass and water for grazing animals; Assisting with transportation of horses; Develop and maintain personal effectiveness.

(b) Optional Units
Any one of the following groups:
Group A–Riding Horses.
Group B–Assisting with horses in harness.
Group C–Assisting with instigation of reproduction; Assisting with parturition care; Assisting with rearing of young stock.

NVQ Racehorse Care Level II

(a) Mandatory Units
Same As Horse Care Level II (above).

(b) Optional Units
Any one of the following groups:
Group A–Handling horses at race meetings; Assisting with preparation of racehorses.
Group B–Assisting with instigation of reproduction; Assisting with parturition care; Assisting with rearing young stock.

NVQ Horse Care Level III – This deals with more complex skills. It indicates that candidates are competent in skilled areas which involve performing a broad range of work activities. This will include many tasks that are complex and non-routine. This level may also indicate the suitability of individuals to supervise others.

NVQ Horse Care Level III

(a) Mandatory Units

Resolving health and condition problems; Monitoring routine care; Transporting horses; Develop teams, individuals and self to enhance performance; Plan, allocate and evaluate work carried out by teams, individuals and self; Create, maintain and enhance working relationships.

(b) Optional Units

Any one of the following groups:
Group A–Preparing horses for work; Riding horses to maintain training.
Group B–Working horses in harness; Driving horses on the road.
Group C–Instigating reproduction; Providing parturition care; Rearing young stock.

(c) Additional Units

Provide grazing and water; Provide trekking opportunities; Improve facilities; Assisting disabled riders.

NVQ Racehorse Care Level III

(a) Mandatory Units

Same As NVQ Horse Care Level III (above).

(b) Optional Units

Any one of the following groups:
Group A–(any two of three units): Preparing horses for work; Preparing horses for racing; Taking horses racing.
Group B–(all three units): Instigating reproduction; Providing parturition care; Rearing young stock.

(c) Additional Units

Provide grazing and water; Improving facilities.

NVQ Horse Care Level IV – This level indicates that a person is competent in the performance of a comprehensive range of skills which may comprise complex, technical or professional expertise. The tasks include planning, design or problem solving activities for which the person has a significant degree of personal responsibility, including suitability to manage and supervise others.

Assessment of competence will be undertaken by a JNHETC Approved Assessor (usually a senior member of staff) with verification from accredited Verifiers attached to an Assessment Centre (usually a managing agent, college, riding school or racing school).

TRAINING OPTIONS

Youth Training Programme

For school leavers where it is available, this is an excellent option. Training leads to the National Vocational Qualification in Horse Care and Management at Levels I to IV (as outlined above). Candidates may also have the option of training for either the BHS, ABRS, NPS and/or BTEC exams. Trainees are given a weekly allowance and may get an accommodation allowance.

You do the bulk of your learning by working at an equestrian centre or training yard under the Youth Training Scheme, and attend college on block- or day-release, where you attend lectures and receive riding tuition. School leaver, Kerry Hutchings opted to train under the Youth Training Programme:

> 'I started riding from the age of eight, and I had my own pony to ride, mostly hacking around the countryside, but that's what initially got me interested in working with horses. I've just started my Youth Training Programme and I am aiming for my BHS Stage I and II exams for the moment; I want to go on to include teaching. Once qualified, I want to work in different areas, expand my skills a bit more, but I'm not quite sure exactly what at the moment,. I'd like to work abroad in a dressage yard, perhaps Germany initially, because that's meant to be the best place for dressage, but I would like to see a bit more of the world.
>
> 'I'm happy with my accommodation and work conditions. The training and instruction here is very good, and I'm also looking forward to my block-release training at college. I am also going to do some training in stud work. I feel the more I can get under my belt, the better.'

However, even under the care of the YT Programme, working with horses is still a tough life. You've got to be very keen to work with horses. You must be prepared for long, irregular hours and not mind working weekends. You must be prepared to work hard and take a lot of interest in the horses – working with animals is easier if you understand them and feel comfortable around them.

As well as performing the daily tasks of a groom, Kerry receives training and instruction with BHSII, Vanessa Cheffing, at Downe Farm Dressage Training Yard:

> 'To make the most of the programme, you have to want to improve your standards and want to get on. If you set high standards for yourself, then you have a better chance of passing exams and getting the kind of well-paid, interesting job that you hope for.'

For more information on Youth Training, contact your local careers office, job centre or the Department of Employment.

NB: Youth Training: There are non-college managing agents who also offer YT. Work is based in a placement yard and one day per week is usually spent at the college or training centre. The work leads to NVQs and trainees get a weekly 'training allowance'. Trainees are entitled to two years on the scheme. The age range starts at sixteen and extends to early twenties. Adult Training Programmes are also available, and are run along similar lines to the Youth Training Programme.

WHERE TO TRAIN

Where you study for your exams will depend upon your own needs and preferences, as well as what is available, but don't compromise your ideals. When choosing a place to train, try to discover the success rate for previous students and, if possible, try to talk to someone who has trained there. An establishment which offers training towards any of the recognised exams should also be approved by the society whose exams they are claiming they can get you through. Training centres vary in the quality and variety of living and training facilities that they offer. It is better to travel some distance to a good training establishment, than to put up with poor training and facilities which will only sicken you of working with horses before you have even begun. You have three options of where to train: at college, at an equestrian centre, or a combination of both.

College Courses

You can attend one of the many colleges that offer courses in all aspects of horse care, riding and management. Most of the college courses are validated either by the National Examining Board for Agriculture, Horticulture and Allied Industries (and is part of the City & Guilds) or by the BTEC. Training can also incorporate either the BHS, ABRS, NPS, BDS, Thoroughbred Industry exams and/or further qualifications. College-based exams at any level tend to include in the course of study considerable preparation for the next level up.

Full-time college training offers the guarantee of regular tuition with a high standard of lecturing and riding instruction. Josephine Tyack BHSPI, trained for her exams at the Duchy College of Agriculture in Cornwall:

> 'Studying at one of the colleges is definitely the cheapest way of getting your BHSPI (British Horse Society Preliminary Instructor), and I believe, the best way. Not only do you get a grant, you may get free accommodation for a year. Because the colleges are not restricted to equestrian students, you'll meet loads of young people and have lots of fun. Your exams are paid for, and the lectures are brilliant because you spend part of the day in the lecture room, and lectures often go way above PI standard.'

However, there are disadvantages to college training, particularly if you have had little or no previous experience of riding, particularly competing. Agricultural colleges don't usually offer the opportunity to compete, and during her exams, Josephine noted that the students who had competed coped fairly well; those who didn't often fell to pieces. 'Some of the girls I was at college with had never competed, so when it came to exams they were nervous wrecks, yet they could ride really well on home ground,' she explains.

Selecting a Horse College

Many of the college courses on offer include training for business studies, including secretarial, computer and book-keeping skills – vital elements if your long-term aims include running your own business. The possibilities are diverse, and most of the colleges will take overseas students, with some providing facilities for disabled students.

Consider the location and the range of courses on offer. If you think that college training will suit your requirements, apply for a prospectus to the colleges that offer the exams that you are eligible to sit. Remember to take into account your long-term aims – you will find that all the colleges vary in the range of training facilities and accommodation on offer. Select at least four colleges.

When you go for an interview, consider first impressions. Do the students seem happy and well-organised? Find out how important horses are to the college; is it just a way of raising student numbers? Consider the level and qualifications of the staff teaching on the horse side and of the management of this part of the college. Inspect the facilities. Chat to the students. Make sure that the college has the most suitable course for you. When you have seen several you can decide how they compare.

This procedure is worthwhile because a college course is a big commitment. Over the last twenty years this route has developed to become the main route into working with horses.

Choosing Your Exam Course

There are a great range of exams offered by the horse industry. The exams you take should reflect the goals you have set for yourself in your career plan. Teaching qualifications are fine if you want to be an instructor, but a waste of time if you want to work as a groom or on a stud farm. Both the BHS and ABRS offer exams specifically aimed at groom's work and those who wish to improve their stable management and riding. The National Pony Society offers an excellent examination system for those interested in stud work. The racing industry also has its own network of exams and training to meet the specific needs of the industry, including stud work and racehorse training.

Whatever other exams you hope to train for, remember that training for the BHS exams will also involve a lot of academic study, as Mary Tyrell, Chief Instructor at the TM International School of Horsemanship in Cornwall points out:

> 'There is a lot of intense study involved in gaining the BHS exams, so if you are not practised in academic work, then you won't cope with your BHS exams either; a lot of youngsters make this mistake. Those still at school who wish to pursue an instructing career should try for as many qualifications as possible in the final years.
>
> 'It's not just riding ability that's assessed. All the muscular,

> skeletal and digestive systems of the horse must be learnt. Not only are the exams hard physical work, but damned hard academic work as well. Also with this type of training, pupils are not "taught" as they are in schools; you've got to learn to read and write about the subject under your own steam. Unless you want to stay at the very lower levels of instructing, you are not going to get very far without GCSE qualifications.'

Whatever exam system you choose, remember that all the British horse industry's qualifications are very highly thought of throughout the world. Although you may have to start off in small yards and riding schools to prove you can work, once you get qualifications and good references then the world is your oyster!

College courses

The Business and Technician Education Council (BTEC) is a national body which caters for those who are attending agricultural or technical colleges for two or three years in order to gain a diploma or higher diploma. The exams include:

BTEC First Diploma: This is a one-year post-school general course, to be called a GNVQ Intermediate Course in the Living Environment. It is a general course in rural studies and personal development with room to specialise in horses. Some first diplomas are pre-farriery courses but not all lead on to reduced apprenticeship time and many of these students will not become farriers.

BTEC National Diploma in Horse Studies: A two-year course (three years in some colleges with a middle, practical sandwich year) to be called an Advanced GNVQ course in the Living Environment. The excellent courses of the early nineties may lose practical content through change to GNVQs.

BTEC Higher National Diploma in Horse Studies: A three-year course with a middle practical sandwich year. It is for those who have studied at advanced level (A levels or a National Diploma or an Advanced Certificate). At some colleges it has a modular structure allowing choice.

BTEC courses can vary in their content and qualifications depending upon which college you attend. It would be advisable to check carefully exactly what each of the colleges are offering by way of training and qualifications gained. Bear in mind your long-term ambitions; e.g. one college may offer courses on accounting or farm management in their curriculum which you realise will be of benefit to your long-term plan of running your own livery yard. Most of the colleges are flexible and may be able to help you devise a training programme to incorporate exams not usually on the equestrian curriculum.

BA (Bachelor of Arts) Degree & Honours Degree, BSc (Bachelor of Science) Degree & Hons. Degree: A few colleges offer specific horse degree courses. Some specialise, such as in overseas markets; some are modular and offer choices; some are particularly strong in management or science.

MSc (Master of Science) or MA (Master of Arts): These higher degrees can also be specific to horses.

The National Examining Board for Agriculture, Horticulture and Allied Industries (NEBAHAI – City & Guilds) is a national body whose exams are college run and may include NVQs and BHS exam training. They are:

NEBAHAI City & Guilds Preliminary Diploma: A one-year course available at only a few colleges. It is designed as a first year course for school leavers. It can include work for NVQs and BHS exams.

NEBAHAI City & Guilds National Certificate in the Management of Horses: A one-year horse course with the accent on skills. It requires a previous year spent on a horse course or in practical work. It can include work for BHS exams and NVQs. (The course at West Oxford is specific to racing and TB work.)

NEBAHAI City & Guilds National Certificate in the Science and Practice of Stud and Stable Husbandry NCMH (Thoroughbred): This will prepare you for suitable employment in a range of occupations associated with racehorses.

NEBAHAI City & Guilds Advanced National Certificate in Equine Business Management (ANCEBM): A one-year course for those with a certificate or BHS Stage II or equivalent, aiming to produce advanced practical and managerial skills which will enable you to take up positions of responsibility or run your own business. At some colleges it may include work towards BHS exams (even up to BHSI level) or specialism in performance development.

College Training – Thoroughbred Breeding and Racing

Several colleges run courses in horse management and husbandry, which form a useful basis from which to approach stud work. The best known of these is held at the West Oxfordshire College at Witney, which is the only college to specialise in training for careers in the Thoroughbred industry, and graduates from here have been welcomed into all sections of the industry.

The college offers three courses aimed at the Thoroughbred industry:

The National Certificate in the Management of Horses (Thoroughbred) is a one-year full-time course in horse husbandry which provides students with all the necessary skills, knowledge and understanding of the care of Thoroughbred horses. The Certificate will give you the opportunity of employment on both Thoroughbred studs and in racing stables. You can also use the training to further your career by obtaining more responsible jobs, or to set up your own enterprise in the equestrian industry.

The course involves intensive teaching in all the skills required on studs and training yards and includes lectures, seminars and office practice which combine to help students balance studies with physical experience in a working situation.

Applicants must be at least 17 years of age on 1st September in the year of entry to the course, have had adequate and appropriate practical experience of working with horses and have had a good general education to GCSE level. Proof is required of an applicant's ability to handle horses through the possession of a nationally recognised horse qualification, or two suitable references. Priority is always given to applicants who have at least one year's full-time work experience with horses.

The BTEC National Diploma in the Management of Thoroughbred Horses is the first and most respected course of its kind which responds to the growing needs of the racehorse training and breeding industry. Increasing investment in high quality bloodstock and major technological advance, have produced an increased demand for employees with the necessary knowledge, skills and administrative flair to fill the many responsible positions in the iIndustry.

It consists of two years based at college, split by a twelve month sandwich period, during which planned work experience is gained in the industry. This period of work experience goes a long way in helping to find work as these days references are a vital accompaniment to college certificates.

Applicants must be at least 17 years of age on 1st September in the year of entry to the course, possess at least 4 GCSE (O Levels) or equivalent at grades A, B or C, preferably including English language, mathematics and a science subject. Prospective students should normally have a minimum of one year's full-time practical experience of working with horses.

The BTEC Higher National Diploma in Business and Finance (Stud and Stable Administration) has been developed by the Stud and Stable Husbandry section of West Oxfordshire College in consultation with the Thoroughbred industry. It has been designed to meet the industry's requirements for: trainers and their assistants, trainers' secretaries, stud managers, stud secretaries, racecourse administrators, managers and administrators in allied and ancillary industries. The course also provides the financial management and skills necessary for those running their own business.

It is a two-year full-time course with three short periods of industrial work experience. The integrated teaching programme is centred around lectures and supported by tutorials, assignments, practical work and work experience.

Applicants must be at least eighteen years of age before the course begins and possess at least one A level pass and three additional GCSEs (or equivalent) at grade C or above. A BTEC National Certificate or Diploma is also acceptable.

Sandwich Courses

Some college courses offer 'sandwich courses' which combine a two-year training programme with one year's practical experience in an equestrian centre, training yard or stud farm, sandwiched between the two year's training. This offers you the chance to put your training into practice and to provide you with a reference that shows you are not only qualified, but also good at your job. As with all training programmes, high passes at college level don't always guarantee you a job. Employers are looking for references as well as qualifications – on paper they know you can do the job, but are you good at it? By doing a sandwich course, you will be able to prove that you are.

CHOOSING A PROFESSIONAL YARD OR EQUESTRIAN CENTRE

Training at a professional yard, such as a stud farm or competition yard, or an equestrian centre offers hands-on experience. As part of the team, you will be directly involved in the day-to-day running of a school, coming into frequent contact with the public which will improve both your communication skills and self-confidence. The high standards set at most professional yards will raise your standards of horsemanship to a level you should adhere to throughout your life.

Few competition yards will allow staff, particularly youngsters to compete and one advantage of training at an equestrian centre is that many will give pupils the opportunity to compete. If you have had little or no experience of riding or competing, you will find training at these centres better in terms of improving self-confidence. Try to find somewhere that will let you get out and compete as much as you can. If you want to pass equestrian exams, you will find it a lot easier if you've competed. It helps get rid of your exam nerves, and it makes you a better rider! Success in exams, as in competing, depends a lot on self-confidence. An equestrian centre also provides plenty of experience of teaching all levels of riders, in all conditions – vital for those wishing to go on to higher exams.

TRAINING ORGANISATIONS

Association of British Riding Schools (ABRS) Being an association of professional proprietors, the ABRS offers an examination structure which is employer-led and concentrates on the practical aspect of working with horses.

The ABRS Preliminary Horse Care and Riding Certificate Levels 1 and 2 is the first step of the qualification ladder. This exam is open to all persons sixteen years and over who are in full-time training or work with horses. The holder of this certificate is fundamentally employable but needs to work under supervision.

The ABRS Groom's Certificate is open to all candidates who have reasonable practical experience in the handling and care of a variety of horses, preferably throughout the four seasons of the year. Holders of this certificate should be capable of basic working on their own, but will require some supervision.

The ABRS Groom's Diploma is intended for those who have a wide knowledge of and experience with a great variety of horses. To sit the exam you must hold the ABRS Groom's Certificate, a current first aid certificate and be at least in your eighteenth year. You must also have had a minimum of two years' full-time occupation/training with horses. A high standard of competence is required for this award. Holders of this diploma are widely recognised and appreciated throughout the horse industry. Honours are awarded to candidates who attain an exceptionally high standard of competence.

Holders of this diploma would be expected to take charge of a yard, work without supervision and organise and supervise other staff.

The ABRS Teaching Certificate is open to persons over the age of seventeen. The holder of this certificate should be good, reliable, pleasant, safety-conscious, caring and competent with a sound knowledge of the subject.

The ABRS Principal's Diploma is their highest examination. It calls for experience in managing a riding school.

Syllabuses and application forms for all the exams are available from the ABRS office (an s.a.e. is required).

The British Driving Society (BDS) represents the interests of driving enthusiasts in Britain. The BDS has proficiency tests in three grades – Preliminary, Intermediate and Advanced – to enable members to confirm their driving ability.

The Preliminary Groom's Test is open to YT students or trainee carriage-driving grooms and requires basic understanding in the care and knowledge of horses equivalent to NVQ Level II.

The Groom's Test requires a very high standard of turn out, harness theory and stable management, and a preliminary standard of driving. This test can lead to a City and Guilds/British Driving Society Diploma. For more information on the society and a syllabus of the tests, contact the secretary at the British Driving Association.

The British Horse Society (BHS) was founded in 1947 and is generally accepted as the leading authority for all horse and pony interests throughout the UK, with the exceptions of hunting, polo and racing. Through its Affiliated Riding Clubs, Pony Clubs and examinations both for horse owners and career students, it aims to improve and maintain standards of riding and horse management.

The BHS offers a structure of examinations that is recognised and admired throughout the world. The exams are run at officially appointed centres throughout the country. The minimum age for entry is sixteen and candidates must be members of the BHS at the time of application. The exam structure is designed to meet the requirements of riding instructors, professional grooms, stable managers and, more recently, those who wish to specialise in the leisure and tourism trade offering trekking and riding holidays. The exams are not geared towards racing or stud work.

The following is a list of the BHS examinations and tests:

The Horse Knowledge and Riding (HK & R) Examinations Stages I and II. If you don't wish to take exams in riding, the Horse Knowledge Riding and Care sections can be taken as separate tests.

The Escort Certificate can be taken if you have passed Stage II of your HK & R. This certificate will show that as a riding escort, you are capable of escorting members of the public riding on the highway.

The Horse Knowledge and Riding Stage III and the *Horse Knowledge and Care Stage III* examination carries a new accolade, The 'Groom's Certificate'.

The Competition Groom's Examination, which may be in a riding or non-riding capacity, meets the specific needs of competition yards and employers. This examination covers the care of competition horses both at home, and in transport by land, sea or air and at shows. The riding aspect will prove your ability to exercise competition horses keeping to a specific exercise programme.

The Preliminary Teaching Certificate examination is open to students who have passed their HK & R Stage II. (A minimum of four GCSEs is required below the age of eighteen; minimum age of entry is seventeen and a half.) This exam, combined with the Horse Knowledge and Riding Stage III exam will give you the title of BHS Preliminary Instructor (which replaces the title of BHS Assistant Instructor).

The Intermediate Stable Manager Certificate (formerly known as the HK & C Stage IV) combined with the Riding Stage IV Certificate and the Intermediate Teaching Certificate will give you the title of Intermediate Instructor.

The Certificate in Equestrian Tourism has three levels: Ride Assistant, Ride Leader and Holiday Centre Manager. The training required for this certificate fills a much needed gap in the tourism and leisure aspect of the horse industry.

Stages I to IV Riding can be taken as separate tests from the horse care, grooming and stable management exams, so if you are only interested in the stable management side of horses you can work your way up the BHS ladder without having to take exams in riding.

The BHS Stable Manager's Examination is the highest exam you can take in a non-riding capacity.

The BHS Equitation/Teaching Examination combined with the Stable Manager's examination will give you the title of BHS Instructor.

The *BHS Fellowship* is the highest award you can receive.

The syllabuses for the above are available from the BHS Examinations

Office (send a large s.a.e. and remittance of 10p each). The Society annually produces a Register of Instructors which guarantees that those listed are qualified, insured and have signed an agreement to a Code of Practice which includes regular up-dating training. The Register includes riding, driving and vaulting Instructors.

The Heavy Horse Committee (HHC) is based at the BHS headquarters in Stoneleigh. It has developed a training programme to cover the basic skills required by those using working horses in forestry, agriculture, haulage work or the leisure and recreation industry. The NVQs include specialist optional units for draught horse work which complement the general units for horse care, e.g. at Level II there is a unit 'Assisting with the Working Horses on the Land' and at Level III there are units 'Working Horses on the Land' and 'Driving Horses on the Road'. 'Driving Horses on the Road' can also be taken as a stand-alone test which offers a certificate of competence. The HHC is also developing a qualification for the trainer/instructor in heavy horse work, as the next step. The NVQs developed by the Heavy Horse Committee have been adapted for use by all grooms and drivers of harness horses.

The Light Harness Horse Board, formed by the British Driving Society and the British Horse Society, examines and qualifies driving instructors – Light Harness Horse Instructors (LHHI).

The National Pony Society (NPS) was founded in 1893 and takes responsibility for Britain's native breeds. The Society has a training route through the National Vocational Qualification in Horse Care and Management, the NPS Assistant Certificate and the NPS Diploma. As with the ABRS exams, the NPS exams are mainly practical – looking after horses is, after all, a practical business. There are no educational qualifications required for the exams, but it is helpful to have basic English, maths and, as the higher exams are for stud work, a basic knowledge of biology.

The NVQs can start from the age of sixteen; they are mostly undertaken at an NPS Approved Training Stud (a list is available from the NPS Secretariat), although students may, if they wish, train at another establishment of their choice. The scheme is based on gathering evidence of competence mostly by observing work on the yard; assessment has to be approved by an assessor to a scheme monitored by the JNHETC. Examinations to test some parts of the syllabus are taken at a number of centres throughout the country each year.

NPS Stud Assistant's Certificate is made up of three parts. Part I is the standard which could be achieved after a few months' training by a school leaver who had no previous training in horse and pony care. Part II is a higher standard, although trainees will continue to require overall supervision and guidance. Part III is higher still and can only be built on Part II. One year's experience is necessary for all candidates for Part III, and he/she must have attained seventeen years to be able to take the examination. Training is undertaken at an NPS Approved Stud.

The NPS Diploma is a professional qualification and is equivalent to NVQ level IV in the levels of Horse Care and Management. To take the Diploma requires a further three years' experience after passing the Stud Assistant's Certificate. The holder of this qualification will be competent as a stud groom and able to manage all stud duties correctly, efficiently and safely, and be left in charge of a stud. A syllabus for the above exams is available from the NPS Secretariat.

Working as a stud assistant includes basic handling, stable routine, grooming, feeding, grass management, health, clothing and saddlery and in some establishments, riding, which may include showing both mounted and in hand.

Management positions in breeding and stud work involve all aspects of general management, getting the mare in foal, foaling, weaning, education and training of the young horse from foal to three years, riding both the young horses and perhaps the stallions, for show purposes. Some will also include preparing and travelling horses for showing, yard management, business management and office skills and procedure.

The Wales Trekking and Riding Association (WTRA) offers those who wish to work in trekking centres the opportunity to take the association's Trek Leader's Certificate which covers the general care and handling of horses, looking after guests and taking out rides. The exam also incorporates the safety aspect of trek leading.

Sources of Information on Training Courses

The ABRS Official Handbook includes the names and addresses of likely employers and training yards.

Where To Ride (available from Kenilworth Press) is the BHS publication that includes the names and addresses of all the BHS approved riding centres throughout the UK and includes the exams they can train you towards.

Where to Train, is another useful BHS publication, which provides more detailed coverage of the various centres offering training for career students.

The Directory of Career Training is compiled and published by the JNHETC. It is updated annually and provides an easy-to-read guide to colleges and equestrian centres that offer training within the horse industry. This directory supplies the name, address, telephone number, awarding organisations and qualifications obtainable of each training establishment.

The NPS includes in its careers information pack a list of the names and addresses of NPS approved training studs which is updated annually.

Contact the appropriate society for more details. Note: There is a charge for the BHS, ABRS and JNHETC publications including post and packing, although these may be available for reference from your careers office or local library. The NPS requires an SAE for its information pack.

Overseas Students

In Britain, many of the colleges and equestrian centres welcome overseas students. Some offer courses in English language, as well as training for the British horse industry's various equestrian based exams. You will not be eligible for the Government-funded schemes such as the Youth Training Scheme, so you will have to pay for your training as well as accommodation, but you may receive financial help from your own Government.

Disabled Students

The opportunities that are available for disabled students who wish to take the various exams on offer within the horse industry depends upon the nature and severity of the disability and the criteria of the exam you wish to take. Because of the physical aspect involved in stud work, racing stables and riding schools, the exams are not suitable for severely disabled people. However, if the nature of your disability is not so severe that you can meet the criteria for the exams, then it will be up to the training centre to which you apply whether they can accommodate you.

The BHS exams also require that you satisfy their insurers, who cover liability during the exams, that you are safe in what you are doing and will not constitute a danger to yourself or the horses in your care.

If you wish to study horses in theory for a career in horse associated work, many of the agricultural colleges offer disabled students the chance to take certain exams covering knowledge of horse care and management. The colleges that offer this also provide excellent facilities for disabled students. Contact the various colleges that offer courses in equine studies to find out which one will best suit your individual requirements.

FARRIERY

Associations

The Worshipful Company of Farriers, established in 1356, is one of the early medieval guilds which, under section one of the Farriers' (Registration) Act 1975, has responsibility for securing adequate standards of competence and conduct among farriers and advancement of the art and science of farriery and education in connection with it.

The Farriers' Registration Council is the governing body of the profession and was established by the Farriers' (Registration) Act 1975, as amended by the Farriers' (Registration) (Amendment) Act 1977. The acts says it is, '...to prevent and avoid suffering by and cruelty to horses arising from the shoeing of horses by unskilled persons, to promote the proper shoeing of horses, to promote the training of farriers and shoeing smiths, to provide for the establishment of a Farriers' Registration Council to register persons engaged in farriery and the shoeing of horses, to prohibit the shoeing of horses by unqualified person, and for purposes connected therewith'.

Through its Investigating and Disciplinary Committees, it exercises a continuing surveillance of professional conduct. The council has also established a managing agency, the Farriery Training Service (FTS), to oversee the training of farriery apprentices in Great Britain. It is responsible for the administration of the terms and conditions set by the FRC for the training of farriery apprentices, including the interview and approval of candidates for apprenticeship, funding for apprenticeships and arranging supervision and training both on and off the job. It liaises with the Worshipful Company of Farriers on examinations and acts as arbiter of all matters relating to the training of farrier apprentices.

Education and Training Courses

Farrier training is moving over to schemes based on National Vocational Qualifications (NVQs); as these come in, changes in training schemes may occur.

You must be at least sixteen years of age; there is no upper age limit. You will need to undergo a medical examination including an eyesight test. If you are under twenty-one, you must have GCSE Grade D passes in four subjects, including English Language or have gained a First Diploma or any certificate equivalent.

Candidates twenty-one years and over who have not achieved the academic requirements must submit a CV to the FTS for consideration.

The training comprises a period of apprenticeship. You must write to an Approved Training Farrier (the FTS publishes a list of ATFs constantly updated, so send off for one when you actually intend to search for employment) in order to find an ATF who is prepared to propose you as a candidate for apprenticeship and employ you throughout.

You may have to live away from home during your training. Candidates cannot apply directly for an apprenticeship, you must be proposed by an ATF. The ATFs have many enquiries each year so you must create a good impression by showing enthusiasm for your work and a willingness to learn. Would-be farriers often write to hundreds of farriers seeking an apprenticeship without success.

Training is either for three years following an approved college 'pre-farriery course', or four years. Both are preceded by a two-month 'probationary period'. The apprenticeship comprises of planned experience gained with the employer (ATF) and includes periods of 'off the job' training at one of the Schools of Farriery.

Terms and conditions of employment for farriery apprentices are jointly approved by the Farriers Registration Council and the National Association of Farriers, Blacksmiths and Agricultural Engineers. Training is grant-aided if you are aged between sixteen and twenty. Funding normally covers accommodation costs and tuition fees while attending a School of Farriery. If you are twenty-one or over, you will not be eligible for grant aid. Therefore, you must be prepared to bear the full cost of your training. However, farriery apprentices are paid a wage.

Apprentices are required to take the *Diploma of the Worshipful Company of Farriers* (DWCF), at the completion of the period of apprenticeship and on passing the DWCF examination, application, together with the appropriate fee, must be made to the FRC before admission to the Registration of Farriers. Once you have passed the DWCF examination and registered with the FRC, you can seek higher qualifications.

Associate of the Worshipful Company of Farriers (AWCF) is an examination which can be taken two years after passing the DWCF, or the finish of apprenticeship, whichever is later. It carries the accolade of the highest technical merit.

The Fellow of the Worshipful Company of Farriers (FWCF) examination can be taken not less than twelve months after obtaining the AWCF, and five years after passing the DWCF, whichever is later. You will be required to submit a thesis on farriery and to lecture on the subject.

SADDLERY

Saddlery Training Courses

Many of today's most successful businesses rely on design as an important tool, and an education in art and design can be the basis of a sound career in industry and commerce. The horse industry is no exception, and horse clothing, accessories, riding boots and fashion riding wear are also things to consider if you wish to study fashion, textiles and leather crafts.

Many people that have worked with horses and have either suffered injuries and are unable to resume their riding careers, or have been made redundant, or simply prefer to ride as a hobby, earn a living from an associated trade and find saddlery a rewarding career, both financially and in terms of job satisfaction. Provided you have good use of arms and hands, both Cambridge and Walsall colleges are open to disabled students and those with special needs. You must inform the relevant centre of your requirement well in advance. All the centres welcome overseas students and mature students; there is no upper age limit on any of the courses.

The standards required for the saddlery trade are specified at four levels:

Level I General basic skills in the use of materials and tools, and the manufacture of simple items of saddlery under supervision.

Level II Specific skills in one of the following: saddlemaking, bridlemaking or harnessmaking, with limited supervision.

Level III Specific skills in two of the following, to a satisfactory standard without supervision: saddlemaking, bridlemaking or harnessmaking.

Level IV Skills at Master Saddler level in saddlemaking, bridlemaking and harnessmaking, to the standards required for the Licentiateship of the City & Guilds of London Institute. This requires the ability to specify tools and supervise the work of others, together with mastery of a range of relevant knowledge and skills, and the ability to apply them.

The three main organisations that run saddlery courses are:

The Cambridge & District Saddlery Courses (International Limited) in Bury St Edmunds, trains students to an exceptionally high standard. All stitching is taught by hand using traditional tools and equipment, the emphasis being on quality not speed. Within the course, pupils are taught the various aspects of leather work. To increase knowledge and improve your chances of employment at a later date, training also includes the making of belts and other leather items.

On completion of the course, you will have the opportunity to establish yourself either at home or at a workshop, on a self-employed basis. The centre offers to take all items of leather goods from you and through a company, sells to many retail outlets; this allows pupils to make as much saddlery as possible, therefore earning a wage. Used as a stop-gap to gain experience, this way you do not leave the establishment without some experience of employment to get you under way. For the self-employed, the Government provides financial help through its Business Start Up programme (see Chapter Seven for more details).

The Cordwainers Technical College in London offers a range of courses in art and design, footwear, manufacture, technology, fashion accessories and leathercrafts, including two full-time saddlery courses run over two years.

The Diploma in Leathercraft and Saddlery covers wide-ranging leather-craft skills combined with design studies, focussing on the design and development of high quality, hand-stitched, solid leathergoods and saddlery. Project based, the course leads you through the initial design concept to the finished product. Experience is divided between the leathercraft and saddlery disciplines, with many of the skills being common to both areas. During the course you will take the City & Guilds certificate exams in both Leathergoods Manufacture and Rural Saddlery at Stages I and II together with the Loriners' Certificate.

The Diploma in Saddlery Studies includes both traditional rural saddlery and modern factory-based production methods. In the first year you will cover all the basic skills and techniques involved and take the City &Guilds Stage I and II Certificate exams. Subjects covered include bridle, harness and saddle making, tack repairs and lorinery. During your second year you can opt to specialise in either bridle and harness making or saddlery. All students take the City & Guilds Stage III Certificate and the Loriners' Certificate exams.

In addition, both courses offer a grounding in business studies and if you achieve the required standards, is it also possible to submit work for assessment by the Guild of Master Craftsmen and to enter for NVQ Saddlery Skills Tests Levels II – IV throughout the course.

Entry requirements for these courses are 4 GCSEs at grade C or above, or a BTEC First Diploma/Certificate or an equivalent qualification. Minimum age is sixteen. If you are not able to attend a two-year course, it may be possible in certain circumstances, to attend the first year and return to study the second year programme at a later date. Free English classes are also provided for students whose first language is not English.

Walsall College of Art in Walsall offers a wide range of programmes in all areas of art and design at several levels, with a proven record of success, over many years, in placing students into work and on to advanced courses, many at university level.

The City & Guilds Bridle & Saddle Course is run from September to July on a full-time basis for two years, although a series of individual programmes can be applied. During the first year, skills tests to Level I and II will be taken. You can arrange a different programme of work, for example, a number of blocks, or even a day-release. There are no formal entry requirements but dexterity, interest and motivation are the qualities required.

You may also wish to diversify into Leathergoods Design and Production. The college offers a two-year course culminating with a BTEC National Diploma. Four GCSEs (at grade C or above) are desired; however, alternative entry requirements would be considered by the course co-ordinator.

After training – where to now?

Initially, your best opportunities for employment will be as a groom or in a riding school or trekking centre. This is the time to put all your training and theory into practice, and to prove that you are not only qualified to look after horses and teach, but that you are hard-working, loyal, conscientious and ready to take on greater responsibilities. Good references from all your previous employers could earn you a lucrative position in the industry. Qualification in any of the horse industry's exams means that you are a professional so you must be professional in all that you do.

Good luck!

Organisations and Addresses

Training Associations

Association of British Riding Schools (ABRS)
Old Brewery Yard, Penzance
Cornwall TR18 2LS
TEL: 01736 69440

British Driving Society (BDS)
27 Dugard Place, Barford
Nr Warwick CV35 8DX
TEL: 01926 62442

The British Horse Society
British Equestrian Centre
Stoneleigh, Kenilworth
Warwickshire CV8 2LR
TEL: 01203 696697

The Joint National Horse Education and Training Council (JNHETC)
Stainton Woodhouse
Lime Kiln Lane, Stainton
Nr Rotherham S66 7QY
TEL: 01709 813458

Riding Clubs
c/o British Horse Society
British Equestrian Centre, Stoneleigh
Kenilworth, Warwickshire CV8 2LR
TEL: 01203 696697

The Pony Club
c/o British Horse Society
British Equestrian Centre, Stoneleigh
Kenilworth, Warwickshire CV8 2LR
TEL: 01203 696697

The National Pony Society (NPS)
Brook House, 25 High Street
Alton, Hants GU34 1AW
TEL: 01420 88333

Riding For the Disabled Association (RDA)
Avenue R, National Agricultural Centre
Kenilworth, Warwickshire CV8 2LR
TEL: 01203 696510

Warwickshire College
Moreton Morrell, Warwick CV35 9LB
TEL: 01926 651367

The Universities and Colleges Admissions Service
Fulton House, Jessop Avenue
Cheltenham, Gloucestershire GL50 3SH
TEL: (for general enquiries) 01242 222444

The Racing Industry

British Racing School
Snailwell Road, Newmarket
Suffolk CB8 7NU
TEL: 01638 665103

Horse Racing Forensic Laboratory Ltd
PO Box 15,Snailwell Road
Newmarket Suffolk CB8 7DT
TEL: 01638 663867

The National Stud
Newmarket, Suffolk CB8 0XE
TEL: 01638 663464

The Thoroughbred Breeders Association (TBA)
Stanstead House, The Avenue
Newmarket, Suffolk CB8 9AA
TEL: 01638 661321

The Jockey Club
42 Portman Square
London W1H 0AP
TEL: 0171 935 2055

The Racing & TB Breeding & Training Board
42 Portman Square
London W1H 0AP
TEL: 0171 935 2055

The National Trainers' Federation
42 Portman Square
London W1H 0AP
TEL: 0171 935 2055

Northern Racing School
Rossington Hall, Great North Road
Doncaster DN11 0HN
TEL: 01302 865462

Weatherbys
Sanders Road, Wellingborough
Northamptonshire NN8 4BX
TEL: 01933 440077

The Horserace Betting Levy Board
52 Grosvenor Gardens
London SW1W 0AU
TEL: 0171 3330043

The Horserace Totalisor Board
Tote House
74 Upper Richmond Road, Putney
London SW15 2SU
TEL: 0181 874 6411

The Stable Lads Association
4 Dunsmore Way, Midway
Swadlincote
Derbyshire DE11 7LA
TEL: 01283 211522

West Oxfordshire College
Holloway Road
Witney, Oxon OX8 7EE
TEL: 01993 703464

Worcester College of Agriculture
Hindlip, Worcester WR3 8SS
TEL: 01905 51591

Associated Trades

The Farriery Training Service
P.O. Box 49, East of England Showground,
Peterborough PE2 OGU
TEL: 01733 234451

Herefordshire College of Technology
Folly Lane, Hereford HR1 1LS
TEL: 01432 352235

The Worshipful Company of Saddlers
Saddlers' Hall, Gutter Lane,
London EC2V 6BR
TEL: 0171 726 8661

Cambridge & District Saddlery Courses
Pinford End Farm House
Pinford End, Hawstead,
Bury St Edmunds
Suffolk IP29 5NU
TEL: 01284 86213

Cordwainers Technical College
Mare Street, Hackney
London E8 3RE
TEL: 0181 985 0237

Walsall Leather Training Centre
56/57 Wisemore, Walsall WS2 8EQ
TEL: 01922 721153

National Council for the Training Of Journalists (for newspaper journalism)
Carlton House, Hemnall Street, Epping
Essex CM16 4NL
TEL: 01378 72395

Periodicals Training Council (for magazine journalism)
Imperial House, 2nd Floor
15/19 Kingsway
London WC2B 6UN
TEL: 0171 836 8798

The Disabled Living Foundation
Harrow Road, London W9
TEL: 0171 289 6111

The Field of Medicine

Chartered Society of Physiotherapy
14 Bedford Row, London WC1R 4ED
TEL: 0171 242 1941

The Faculty of Homeopathy
Royal London Homeopathic Hospital
London WC1N 3HR
TEL: 0171 837 2495

The McTimoney Chiropractic School
14 Park End Street, Oxford OX1 1HH
TEL: 01865 246786

Royal College of Veterinary Surgeons (RCVS)
32 Belgrave Square, London SW1X 8QP
TEL: 0171 235 4971

Self-Employment

The Princes Youth Business Trust
5 Cleveland Place, London SW1Y 6JJ
TEL: 0171 321 6500

Rural Development Commission
11 Cowley Street, London SW1P 3NA
TEL: 0171 2766969

The Highlands and Islands Development Board
Bridge House, 27 Bank Street
Inverness IV1 1QR
TEL: 01463 234171

The Development Board for Rural Wales
Ladywell House, Newtown
Powys SY16 1JB
TEL: 01686 626965

Recommended Reading

ABRS Official Handbook, ABRS.
BHS Manual of Equitation, Kenilworth Press.
BHS Manual of Horsemanship, BHS.
Bromiley, Mary, *Equine Injury and Therapy,* Blackwell Scientific.
Devereux, Sue & Liz Morrison, *Veterinary Care of the Horse,* J.A. Allen.
French, Jo, *BHSAI Course Companion,* J.A. Allen.
German National Equestrian Federation, *Advanced Techniques of Riding,* Kenilworth Press.
German National Equestrian Federation, *Principles of Riding,* Kenilworth Press.
Houghton-Brown, Jeremy, *Horse Care,* Blackwell Scientific.
Houghton-Brown, J & V Powell-Smith, *Horse Business Management,* Blackwell Scientific.
Houghton-Brown, J & V Powell-Smith, *Horse and Stable Management,* Blackwell Scientific.
McBane, Susan, *Illustrated Guide To Horse Tack,* David and Charles.
Mortimer, Monty, *Competition Training For Horse and Rider,* J.A. Allen.
Mortimer, Monty, *Riding Instructor's Handbook,* David and Charles.
Pilliner, Sarah, *Horse Nutrition and Feeding,* Blackwell Scientific.
Rose, John & Sarah Pilliner, *Practical Stud Management,* Blackwell Scientific.
Sivewright, Molly, *Thinking Riding,* J.A. Allen.

Index

ABRS *see* Association of British Riding Schools
ABRS official handbook 148
Accommodation 29-31, 109-10
Accounting 13-14 *see also* Book-keeping
Adult Training Programme 137
Advertising 13, 57, 125-7
Adverts, Job 103-5
Agricultural colleges 10
Alternative therapy 94-102
Animal Health Clinic, Newmarket 87
Applying for a job 105-8
Apprenticeship, Racing 73
Army 58
Assistant trainer 78-9
Association of British Riding Schools (ABRS) tests 12, 136, 138-9, 139,144-5
Association of Chartered Physiotherapists in Animal Therapy 100
Association of Farriers, Blacksmiths and Agricultural Engineers 151

BDS *see* British Driving Society
Bloodstock agencies 82-3
Book-keeping 13-14, 83, 125
Books 49, 57, 120 *see also* Journalism, Magazines, Publishing, Writing
British Driving Society (BDS) 35, 138, 145, 147-8
British Equestrian Federation 46
British Franchise Association (BFA) 116
British Horse Society (BHS) 136, 138-9, 145-7, exams and qualifications 51, 53, 149, tests 12
British Horseracing Board (BHB) 64-5, 74
British Racing School, Newmarket 65, 68
Budgeting in business 120, 126
BUNA Camp 54
Business and Technical Education Council (BTEC) 140-2
Business planning 119-20
Business Start-up programme 118, 125, 153

Cambridge and District Saddlery Courses (International Ltd.) 152-3
Career Development Loan 56
Career planning 9-18
Careers office 137
Choosing a yard or centre 143-4
City and Guilds 62, 138, 153-4
College courses 55, 137-43
Colleges, agricultural 10, art 58, horse 138-9
Communication skills 20, 82
Competition rider 44-50, yard 143
Computer skills 62-3, 82-3
Conditions of work 54
Conduct, Rules of 111
Contract of employment 33, 111-13
Courses, degree 59, 141, exam 139-43
Curriculum vitae (CV) 14, 63, 105-9, 150
CV *see* Curriculum vitae

Days off 111
Dealing 127-30
Dealing yard groom 34
Degree courses 59, 141
Dentistry, Horse 85, 101-2
Department of Employment 56, 118, 137
Department of Social Security 115
Development Board for Rural Wales 119
Directory of Career Training 149
Directory of Grants and Trusts 125
Disabled Living Foundation 117
Disabled students 149, 152
Disablement Resettlement Officer 117
Distribution profile 125
Dress 108
Dressage groom 34-5
Driver, Horse box 78
Driving groom 35
Duchy College of Agriculture 138

Education 55 *see also* Projects, Schoolwork
Employment, Contract of 33, 111-13
Employment agencies
Enterprise agencies 117-18
Equestrian centres 10, 144
Equestrian tourism and leisure 23-4

Equine dentistry 85, 101-2
European Union 50-5, 88, 127
Eventing 47
Eventing groom 35-6
Exam courses 139-43
Exams 13-14

Faculty of Homeopathy, London 94
Farriers' Registration Council 149-51
Farriery 56, 149-51
Farriery Training Service (FTS) 150
Federation Equestre International 46
Finance 44, 47, 55-6, 124-5
Franchising 116-17
Freelance employment 22-3, 57, 114

GCSE 55, 87, 90, 96, 100, 140, 142-3, 150, 153-4
Groom 10-12, 24-43, dealing yard 24, dressage 34-5, driving 35, eventing 35-6, hunt 36-8, polo 38-40, showing 40, show jumping 41-2

Highlands and Islands Development Board 119
Holiday entitlement 33, 111, pay 33
Holiday riding centres 124
Horse and Hound 16, 52, , 63, 103, 121
Horse associated trades 10, 55-63
Horse dentistry 85, 101-2
Horserace Betting Levy Board 66, 83
Horserace Totalisator Board 66
Horseracing Forensic Laboratory Ltd. 83
Hours of work 31-2
Hunt groom 36-8

Inland Revenue 115
Instructor, Riding 19-24
Insurance, 113, medical 53-4, public liability 54-5
International competitions 49-50
Interview 108-10

JNHETC *see* Joint National Horse Education and Training Council
Job, adverts 103-5, applying for a 105-8, centre 137, description 110, 112-13
Jockey 67, 73-4
Jockey Club 64-6, 83-4
Joint National Horse Education and Training Council (JNHETC) 62, 69, 132-3, 148

Journalism 56-8, 84 *see also* Books, Magazines, Publishing, Writing

Kompass directory 45, 125

Laboratory work 83
Life insurance 113
Loan, Bank 124-5
Local authorities 118
Location of business 124
Loriners' Certificate 153

Magazines 48, 57 *see also* Books, Journalism, Publishing, Writing
Marketing 59-61, 88, 121-3, consultant 60-1, 123, strategy 129-31
Mathematics 14
Medical insurance 53-4
Medicine 85-102
National Council for Vocational Qualifications (NCVQ) 62, 65, 69-70, 132-7, 150, 153

National Examining Board for Agriculture, Horticulture and Allied Industries (City & Guilds) 138
National Insurance 29, 33, 52
National Pony Society (NPS) exams 25, 136,138-9, 147-8
National Stud, Newmarket 81
National Trainers' Federation 68, 83
NCVQ *see* National Council for Vocational Qualifications
Newspapers local 103, 126
Non-Thoroughbred industry 9-10, 28
Northern Racing School, Doncaster 71

Olympic Games 42, 49-50
Open University 55
Overseas students 21, 149
Own business 114
Oxfordshire School of Chiropractors 96

Partnership 115-16
Periodicals 126 *see also* Magazines
Personal qualities for marketing 60, for vet 91-3
Pharmaceutical companies 88
Photography 57-8
Physical education 14
Physiotherapy 99-101
Planning a career 9-18, in business 125
Police, mounted 58

Polo groom 38-40
Prince's Youth Business Trust (PYBT) 117-18, 127
Profit and loss chart 125
Projects 14 *see also* Education, Schoolwork
Public liability insurance 54-5
Publishing 56-8 *see also* Magazines, Books, Writing

Qualifications, 24-5, 51 *see also* Association of British Riding Schools, British Horse Society, Business and Technical Education Council, Courses, Exams, Joint National Horse Education and Training Council, National Council for Vocational Qualifications, National Pony Society

Racecourse work 83
Racing and Thoroughbred Breeding Training Board (RTBT) 65, 69, 74
Racing Employment register 84
Racing industry 19-10, 28, 64-84, 114
Racing schools 70-4
Racing yards 124
Recruitment in racing 68
Retailing 61-2 *see also* Sales staff
Riding for the Disabled 100
Riding instructor 19-24
Riding school 11, 124
Royal College of Veterinary Surgeons 86, 89, 92-3
Rules of conduct 111
Rural Development Commission (RDC) 117-18, 127

Saddlery 62, 151-4
Sales staff 57, 61-2, 88
Sandwich courses 143
School of McTimoney Chiropractic 85, 95-9
Schoolwork 13-14 *see also* Education, Projects
Scottish Development Agency 119
Scottish Vocational and Education Council (SCOTVEC) 132
Secretarial work 63, 66, 83-4
Security work 83
SEDAN 52
Self-employed marketing 60, 114-31
Show jumping groom 41-2
Showing groom 40
Society of Master Saddlers 62
Sole trader 115
Sponsorship 45-8
Sponsorship directory 25, 46
Stable husbandry 28
Stable lad 67-8, 75-8
Stable Lads Association (SLA) 66-7, 74
Stud management 28
Stud work 81-2, 124, 141, 143

Thoroughbred Breeders' Association (TBA) 65-6
Thoroughbred industry 9-10, 28, 81-2, 141-3 *see also* Racing industry, Stud work
Time off 31-2
Tourism, Equestrian 23-4
Trade stands 126
Trainers, 22-3, 124, racing 78-80
Training, Career 24-8, 69-70, 132-54
Training organisations 144-54
Travel arrangements 109-11
Travelling lad 78
Travelling opportunities 42-3
Trekking 23

Veterinary hospitals 93, nursing 86-9, surgeon 89-93, work 14, 85-102

Wages 29-30, 54, 109-11
Wales Trekking and Riding Association 148
Walsall College of Art 153
Warwickshire College 83
Weatherbys 66
West Oxfordshire College 141-2
Where to Ride 148
Where to Train 148
Worcester College of Agriculture 70
Work permit 54
Working abroad 50-5
Worshipful Company of Farriers 149
Worshipful Company of Saddlers 62
Writing 13, 48-9 *see also* Books, Journalism, Magazines, Publishing

Yellow pages 126
Youth Training Programme (racing) 70, 136-7
Youth Training Scheme (YTS) 58, 65